At The Going Down Of The Sun

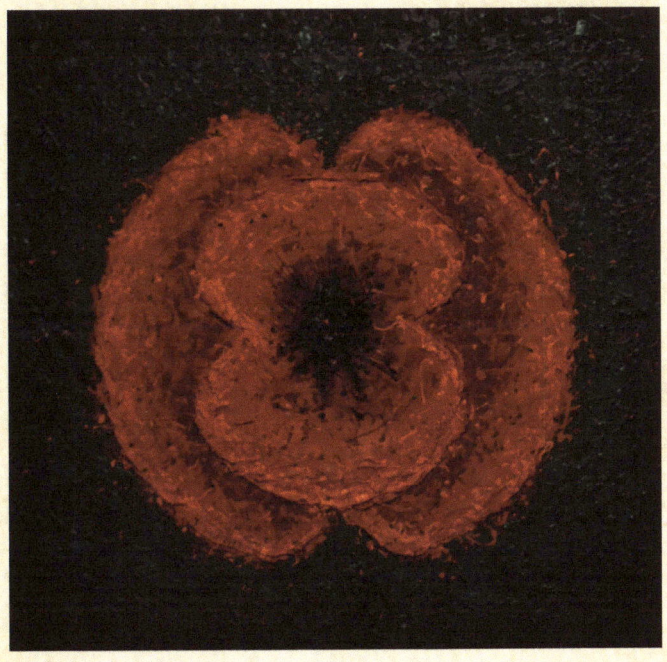

by
Richard Savage and Marian Savill

Savage

Publications

ISBN 978-1-912768-80-6

Original text copyright 2014 Richard Savage and Marian Savill
Illustration and original artwork copyright 2014 Richard Savage and Marian Savill

All rights reserved.
No part of this book may be used or reproduced
in any manner whatsoever without written permission,
except in the case of brief quotations embodied in
critical articles or reviews.

Published 2014 by Savage Publications

All world wide rights reserved

In the making of this book we have endeavoured to contact and credit any potential owners of images and text. Due to the age of the material it has not always been possible to find. Should anyone reading this book have information regarding the ownership of the images please contact us and we will revise future editions of this publication

Copyright Disclaimer Under Section 107 of the Copyright Act 1976, allowance is made for fair use for purposes such as criticism, comment, news reporting, teaching, scholarship, and research. Fair use is a use permitted by copyright statute that might otherwise be infringing. Non-profit, educational or personal use tips the balance in favour of fair use.

A Friend Remembered by Richard Savage

Foreword

Since man grasped a burnt stick and pressed it upon a surface, he has sought to express himself artistically. From cave painting to Photoshop, he has tried to make sense of the world around him and express his feelings about the events of the time. All the joy and love, passion and frustration, their *joie de vivre*. Art has been used as a force for good and peace, though the flip side of the coin is that it has also been used as a tool to oppress, demonise and manipulate people.

Radically different to any other book you have ever read on the subject of World War One, we invite you to take a very personal journey with the artists and authors, Richard Savage and Marian Savill, as they explore the global conflict of the First World War through their artwork. As artists, they share their unique perspective on the events and facts surrounding the war, both as individual artists and through their collaborative pieces. As authors, during the research, Richard and Marian have been drawn into the historical stories of the war, sometimes evoking deep rooted emotions about the people involved in the conflict and they have been astounded at the realities, truth being stranger than fiction.

Page after page you will find thought provoking art and reflections on the events of the Great War. Richard and Marian are not historians, the subject matter simply gripped them, as we are sure it will grip you. You will find the content captivating and accessible. No matter what age you are, there is something for everyone in this book.

In Flanders Fields by Marian Savill

Richard dislikes being pigeonholed into a category or medium, choosing to explore his own creativity in his own way. Espresso fuels his lifelong love affair with paints and pencils. He never really knows where his next idea will spring from; an image or concept will grab him and he pursues it with a passion.

Learning how to use light is key, then follows tone, form, contrast and colour. Richard spends hours on each piece, creating a moment in time on the canvas, building the story in paint. The detail and atmosphere have the ability to draw you in to his artwork. Richard adores what he does and this comes through in his work.

Marian works almost exclusively with used materials to create assemblage, collage and jewellery pieces. She has a very tactile working process; gathering, arranging and rearranging potential components to reach the point of being able to begin the physical assembly of a piece of artwork. Even then, the construction process is organic and continually evolves as elements are brought in, taken out or altered during the assembly of the work.

Marian has a multifaceted art career; she exhibits locally, nationally and internationally, is a director of a youth arts organisation and delivers workshops and Arts Award to children and young people.

Our working methods are very individual. Richard comes from a fine art and illustration background, his work is characterised by its detail, and requires little or no explanation. Marian has a freer more abstract style in both assemblage and collage pieces and we feel it would be helpful to explain some of the thinking processes behind Marian's work. Our joint work is partly painted in a naïve style and an adaptation of the methods first used by Jackson Pollock in the 1950s, this kinetic work captures the feeling, moment and energy of the scene before us.

Although our individual styles are very different, this book has been created and compiled by us both. Most of the views expressed are our joint view so we have not felt the need to attribute the text to either one of us, however there are areas where we have worked alone and, where we have, we indicate this in the text with either **MS** or **RS**.

We work, at times, in the same studio and this book instinctively evolved from mutual ideas. World War One seemed such a natural subject for us to explore as artists and we both felt, right from the start, that we had something to say and a desire to share it with a wider audience. We both had relatives who served in the war and it has left its mark on both of our families as it has millions of others. That is the premise of the book; ordinary everyday people, caught up in extraordinary circumstances, doing exceptional things, or not. It is important to remember that not everyone who served was a hero, not everyone wanted to go with a song in their heart, every story is very individual.

We have chosen to include a variety of media for this book. In addition to our own art work we wanted to explore the artwork of others in posters and photographs which we hope you will agree gives a feel for the time.

We have in no way tried to write an authoritative history of the First World War, we are *not* historians. No one book could realistically contain the wealth of information on this subject. This book is from our personal perspective, as artists, on the things that have inspired us to produce this body of work.

We very much hope this book will spring board you into your own exploration of the events surrounding the First World War and how it shaped the lives of all our families.

She was saying goodbye and she didn't even know it.

Markus Zusak

Like so many things, an incident that seems quite unrelated to an event can have consequences. In chaos theory, Edward Lorenz coined the phrase *butterfly effect*, which is when a single event, however small, can change the course of events widely and forever.

Gavrilo Princip, a Bosnian born Serb intent on striking a blow for the integration of his people into Greater Serbia, was one of a group who plotted to kill Archduke Franz Ferdinand of Austria in 1914. His comrade's attempts failed but, by chance, Princep came upon his target whilst buying a sandwich in a deli. He takes his chance, kills the Archduke and thereby starts a chain of fateful world events.

A long series of political skirmishes in the decades preceding the assassination of the Archduke Ferdinand gave rise to the cascading chain of events which destabilised Europe which, in turn, gave the opportunity to Kaiser Wilhelm to forward his ambitions for a larger German empire. Britain declared war on Germany on 4th August 1914.

The ensuing conflict cost over 16 million deaths and 20 million wounded, the decimated flower of a generation.

MS I found the story of Gavrilo Princep and his sandwich very captivating. Whether it is apocryphal or not, I wanted to create a piece centred around the tale. The idea that something as innocuous as a sandwich could possibly be held responsible for such a devastating global event is almost beyond comprehension and holds a grim fascination for me. Towards the end of the creation of this collage piece a line of text in the randomly assembled background caught my eye and became the serendipitously appropriate title of the piece, *He Dined Rather Hastily*.

He Dined Rather Hastily by Marian Savill

Above, one of the many original war time recruiting posters. While the poster, top right, featuring Lord Kitchener is an enduring and iconic image, it was originally designed by Alfred Leete as a cover for the magazine, *London Opinion*, and there are discrepancies as to whether it was ever actually used as a poster during the war.

While considering our collaborative artwork several pieces sprung immediately to mind. The first was *At the Going Down of the Sun*, the classic poppy image for the book cover but the second was undoubtedly the iconic image of Lord Kitchener.

Kitchener was drowned when HMS Hampshire struck a mine off the Orkney Islands on 5th June 1916.

What Price Your Country's Call? by Richard Savage and Marian Savill

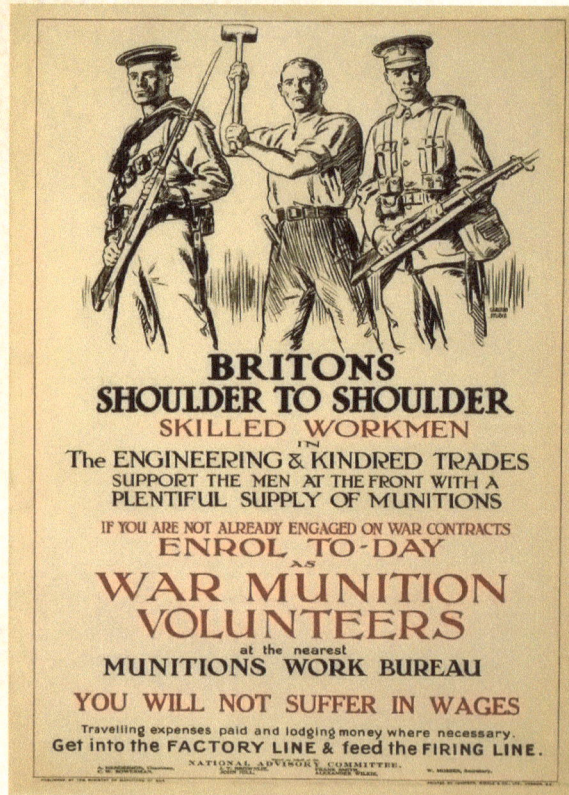
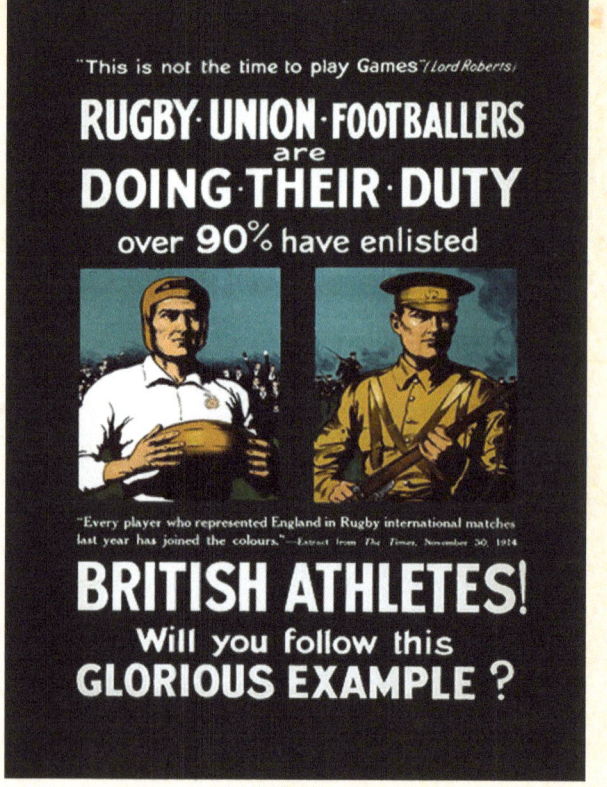

Gang zum Schützengraben

Durch Granattrichter,
Schmutzige Pfützen,
Stapfen sie.
Über Soldaten,
Frierend im Erdloch,
Stolpern sie.

Ratten huschen pfeifend übern Weg,
Sturmregen klopft mit Totenfingern
An faulende Türen
Leuchtraketen
Pestlaternen . . .

Zum Graben zum Graben.

Ernst Toller

The Road to the Trenches

Through grenade furrows
And filthy puddles
They walk.
Over soldiers
Freezing in a hole in the ground
They stagger.

Rats dart squeaking over their path
Stormy rain knocks with fingers of death
On decaying doors
Signal rockets
Plague lanterns…

From trench to trench.

Ernst Toller
Translated by Peter Appelbaum

Marching - As Seen from the Left File

My eyes catch ruddy necks
Sturdily pressed back -
All a red brick moving glint.
Like flaming pendulums, hands
Swing across the khaki -
Mustard-coloured khaki -
To the automatic feet.
We husband the ancient glory
In these bared necks and hands.
Not broke is the forge of Mars;
But a subtler brain beats iron
To shoe the hoofs of death,
Who paws dynamic air now.
Blind fingers loose an iron cloud
To rain immortal darkness
On strong eyes.

Isaac Rosenberg

Unending Future by Marian Savill

The campaign started with a spirit of optimism but quickly descended into an entrenched stalemate. It was estimated for every mile of front line there would be at least 40 miles of trenches. These were dug and zigzagged across the Western Front. An infantry officer's average life expectancy while in the trenches was six weeks. Most at risk of early death in the trenches were the junior officers and the stretcher bearers.

Both sides were stuck in a quagmire of filth and rats. There were millions of rats along the front line. A pair of rodents could produce as many as 900 young a year in trench conditions so soldiers attempts to kill them were futile. Rats frequently ran over sleeping men in the trenches and also gnawed on the rotting corpses of fallen soldiers in no man's land.

Many thousands of foreign labourers, were employed behind the lines, working in the ports, roads and on the railways. This freed up men to serve in combat roles in other theatres of war.

On Somme

Suddenly into the still air burst thudding
And thudding and cold fear possessed me all,
On the gray slopes there, where Winter in sullen brooding
Hung between height and depth of the ugly fall
Of Heaven to earth; and the thudding was illness own.
But still a hope I kept that were we there going over
I, in the line, I should not fail, but take recover
From others courage, and not as coward be known.
No flame we saw, the noise and the dread alone
Was battle to us; men were enduring there such
And such things, in wire tangled, to shatters blown.
Courage kept, but ready to vanish at first touch.
Fear, but just held. Poets were luckier once
In the hot fray swallowed and some magnificence.

Ivor Gurney

Hawthown redoubt mine at Beaumont Hamel

The Battle of the Somme started on 1st July 1916 at 7:28 am when the Lochnagar mine was detonated. The mine was created by the Royal Engineers and was located south of La Boisselle. The mine contained approximately 60,000 lbs of ammonal. A second mine, known as the Y Sap mine, and several other mines were set off simultaneously. The explosions were intended to weaken the German strong points prior to the allied offensive.

British infantry waiting to attack were struck by falling debris and one man, having braced himself in a trench, had his leg broken by the shock wave.

On the first day of the Battle of the Somme, the British Army suffered approximately 60,000 casualties of whom 20,000 were fatalities. It was the worst toll within a day in the whole of British military history. Sixty percent of officers involved on the day were killed.

A witness from the air, 2nd Lieutenant C.A. Lewis of No. 3 Squadron RFC, said, *The whole earth heaved and flashed, a tremendous and magnificent column rose up in the sky. There was an ear-splitting roar drowning all the guns, flinging the machine sideways in the repercussing air. The earth column rose higher and higher to almost 4,000 feet. There it hung, or seemed to hang, for a moment in the air, like the silhouette of some great cypress tree, then fell away in a widening cone of dust and debris.*

Lochnagar crater as it can be seen today.

The scale of explosives used in the war was staggering. The density of the shell craters altered the geography of the land and many of the scars to the landscape can be seen to this day. The vast amount of munitions used was such that no accurate numbers can be given, but it is estimated that more than a billion shells were fired and as many as 30 percent of the larger calibre shells failed to explode and many also contained poison gas.

A century after the war, thousands of unexploded shells, mortar bombs and grenades, known as *iron harvest*, are still found on the former front lines. It is the job of DOVO, Belgium's bomb disposal unit, to find and make the explosives safe. They still recover between 150 and 200 tons each year and it is not without risk - over 20 members of the unit have been killed since it was formed in 1919.

Seen above and below, before and after aerial photographs showing the complete devastation of the terrain over which the Battle of Passchendaele was fought.

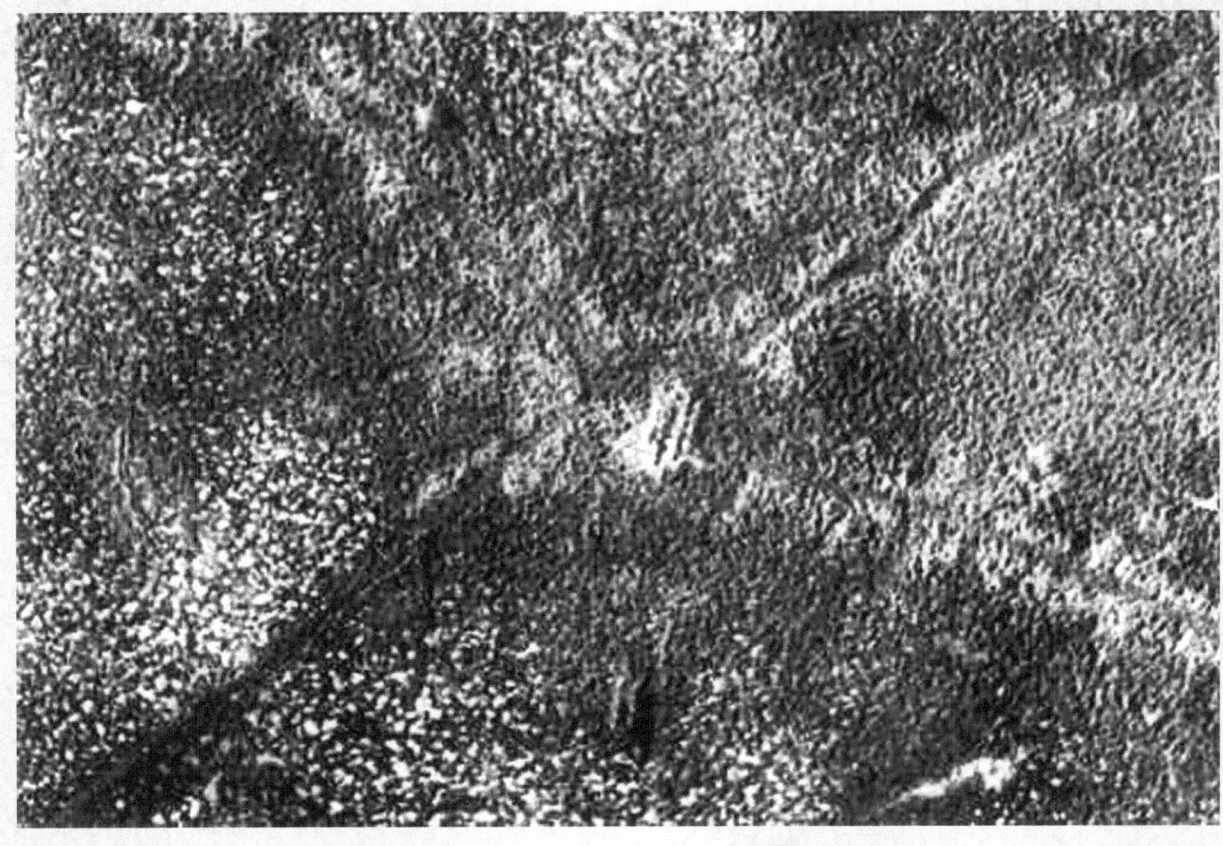

Seen above, one of many images that inspired a series of collaborative paintings we have entitled Tortured Landscapes. We wanted to explore the wholesale destruction of the land in paint, looking at form and movement. The resulting desolate panoramic vistas are powerful and made more striking by their simplicity.

Searching with Weary Eyes by Marian Savill

MS The upcycled wood frame of this piece immediately suggested to me a vista of no man's land seen through a trench periscope. My paternal grandfather fought in the war. Not uncommon amongst survivors, he very rarely spoke of his experiences in the trenches and it is unimaginable to me how his eighteen year old self must have felt looking out over the devastation of no man's land. The artwork is best viewed at eye level, the impact of the full vista evoking a sense of chilling foreboding.

The war had a huge environmental impact; the use of chemical weapons for the first time in warfare caused soil erosion, deforestation and water contamination on a massive scale. Miles of trenches cut across the landscape and heavy artillery bombardment crippled French agriculture. Nearly half a million acres of forest were destroyed during the conflict and animal populations were severely affected by the war, some were pushed to the brink of extinction. As a title, *The Wail of the Forest*, suggested to me an imagined outpouring of arboreal grief, trees are the life blood of the landscape and I wanted to capture something of this enormous environmental loss.

The Wail of the Forest by Marian Savill

A collection of trench scenes; above, two scenes show German soldiers in the trenches, below, British and German soldiers sharing a cigarette in no man's land. Like so many pictures this last one is staged after the event due to the practicalities of combat. The German soldier is most probably a prisoner of war, due to his lack of equipment.

And then the Rain Began by Marian Savill

MS The weather conditions on the Western Front during the war are well documented, the filthy liquid mud and water that men stood in for hours on end in the trenches was responsible for much ill health. Thousands of men tramping over wet ground soon turned the land into a quagmire of unimaginable proportions. *And then the Rain Began,* a collage of mono-printed papers on wood, was inspired by a line from the poem, *Counter Attack,* by Siegfried Sassoon. The piece gives an abstracted feeling of driving rain, evocative of the conditions of the battlefield.

Seen left, a Medical Officer inspects men's feet for trench foot, a dreadful condition caused by prolonged exposure to damp and cold conditions. Feet could have a decaying odour. As the condition worsens, the feet begin to swell and, in the advanced stages, blisters and open sores, lead to fungal infections. Left untreated, trench foot cases resulted in gangrene, which often led to amputation.

The trenches had an appalling smell; a combination of rotting flesh, overflowing latrines, unwashed bodies, disinfectant, cordite and gas. They were a powerful assault on the sense of smell, an aroma that no one who spent time there would ever forget.

Anthem for Doomed Youth

What passing-bells for these who die as cattle?
Only the monstrous anger of the guns.
Only the stuttering rifles' rapid rattle
Can patter out their hasty orisons.
No mockeries for them from prayers or bells,
Nor any voice of mourning save the choirs,-
The shrill, demented choirs of wailing shells;
And bugles calling for them from sad shires.

What candles may be held to speed them all?
Not in the hands of boys but in their eyes
Shall shine the holy glimmers of goodbyes.
The pallor of girls' brows shall be their pall;
Their flowers the tenderness of silent minds,
And each slow dusk a drawing-down of blinds.

Wilfred Owen

Above, an allied soldier composing a letter in a *funk hole*, a term popularised during the war. To be in a funk was to be in a low mood or want to hide away; funk holes were openings cut in the trench walls where soldiers could retire when not on duty.

Left, a group of well equipped German sentries prepare to enter the line, each wearing a Stirnpanzer affixed to the front of their M1916 Stahlhelme. The Stirnpanzer was a 4mm thick steel plate weighing about 4kg, designed to be mounted on the front of the steel helmet from late 1916 onwards.

Stay Thy Weary Feet by Marian Savill

MS For me, working with unconventional materials, discovering their artistic potency, is always an exciting challenge. I have worked extensively with video tape and, knowing I wanted to create faux barbed wire for *Stay Thy Weary Feet* and *Before the Brazen Frenzy Begins*, I knew it would be the perfect material. Initially, I carefully stretched it and then painstakingly knotted it before adding it to the work to create the barbed wire effect. All of the elements in both these pieces of work have all had a previous life; book covers, photographs, old tin, poetry text, video tape. Working with life worn objects holds a fascination for me, they have an aged beauty, a distinctive individuality, which I try to enhance and celebrate in my work.

Before the Brazen Frenzy Begins by Marian Savill

Cramped in that Funnelled Hole

Cramped in that funnelled hole, they watched the dawn
Open a jagged rim around; a yawn
Of death's jaws, which had all but swallowed them
Stuck in the bottom of his throat of phlegm.
They were in one of many mouths of Hell
Not seen of seers in visions, only felt
As teeth of traps; when bones and the dead are smelt
Under the mud where long ago they fell
Mixed with the sour sharp odour of the shell.

Wilfred Owen

Louse Hunting

Nudes - stark aglisten,
Yelling in lurid glee. Grinning faces of fiends
And raging limbs
Whirl over the floor one fire.
For a shirt verminously busy
Yon soldier tore from his throat
With oaths
Godhead might shrink at, but not the lice.
And soon the shirt was aflare
Over the candle he'd lit while we lay.
Then we all sprang up and stript
To hunt the verminous brood.
Soon like a demons' pantomine
The place was raging.
See the silhouettes agape,
See the gibbering shadows
Mixed with the battled arms on the wall.
See gargantuan hooked fingers
Dug in supreme flesh
To smutch supreme littleness.
See the merry limbs in hot Highland fling
Because some wizard vermin
Charmed from the quiet this revel
When our ears were half lulled
By the dark music
Blown from Sleep's trumpet.

                                Isaac Rosenberg

A Demons' Pantomime by Marian Savill

MS Lice were a huge problem in the trenches and must have been intensely annoying to say the very least. A common occupation for soldiers was *chatting*, where men would sit together and remove lice from their uniforms, often running a candle flame along the seams to eradicate the beasts. Isaac Rosenberg's poem, *Louse Hunting*, describes the experience with such evocative candour and was my inspiration for *A Demons' Pantomime*.

In the trenches, between fighting, all the minutiae of daily life went on. Cooking, eating and bodily functions needed to be taken into consideration. There were also activities more associated with trench life such as caring for feet to avoid trench foot, hunting rats and delousing.

July 1st, 1916

       A soft grey mist,
Poppies flamed brilliant where the woodlands bend
Or straggling in amongst the ripening corn,
       Green grass dew kist;
While distantly a lark's pure notes ascend,
       Greeting the morn.

       A shuddering night;
Flames, not of poppies, cleave the quivering air,
The corn is razed, the twisted trees are dead;
       War in his might
Has passed; Nature lies prostrate there
       Stunned by his tread.

       Aimee Byng Scott

One of the unusual things we found while we researched aspects of the Western Front were sniper trees, or Observational Post Trees. Royal Engineers would select a strategically placed tree; ideally large and dead, potentially bomb blasted. It would be photographed, sketched and measured in situ. Then, in a workshop behind the lines, artists and engineers would construct an exact replica made from steel cylinders and reinforced with scaffolding. The structure was then painted and camouflaged to resemble the original tree. During the night, the original tree would be replaced with the new version, ready for a sniper or observer to occupy.

All the Roads Lead to Blackest Carrion by Marian Savill

MS A lot of my artwork is prompted by words; poetry, song lyrics, quotes. I'm an avid reader and collect words, snippets of conversations and interesting etymological fragments. Whilst researching Austrian poet, George Trakl, I came across various translations of his poem, Grodek, but Michael's Hamburger's version using the phrase *all the roads lead to blackest carrion* particularly grabbed my attention. I've always been fascinated by symbols in art, and many birds have been symbolically featured in paintings throughout history. Crows and ravens are often seen as heralds of death and destruction, portentous of impending danger, and the carrion line from Grodek is a perfect fit for this ominous collage piece.

Grodek

Am Abend tönen die herbstlichen Wälder
Von tödlichen Waffen, die goldnen Ebenen
Und blauen Seen, darüber die Sonne
Düstrer hinrollt; umfängt die Nacht
Sterbende Krieger, die wilde Klage
Ihrer zerbrochenen Münder.
Doch stille sammelt im Weidengrund
Rotes Gewölk, darin ein zürnender Gott wohnt
Das vergoßne Blut sich, mondne Kühle;
Alle Straßen münden in schwarze Verwesung.
Unter goldnem Gezweig der Nacht und Sternen
Es schwankt der Schwester Schatten durch den schweigenden Hain,
Zu grüßen die Geister der Helden, die blutenden Häupter;
Und leise tönen im Rohr die dunklen Flöten des Herbstes.
O stolzere Trauer! ihr ehernen Altäre
Die heiße Flamme des Geistes nährt heute ein gewaltiger Schmerz,
Die ungeborenen Enkel.

            Georg Trakl

At nightfall the autumn woods cry out
With deadly weapons and the golden plains,
The deep blue lakes, above which more darkly
Rolls the sun; the night embraces
Dying warriors, the wild lament
Of their broken mouths.
But quietly there in the willow dell
Red clouds in which an angry god resides,
The shed blood gathers, lunar coolness.
All the roads lead to blackest carrion.
Under golden twigs of the night and stars
The sister's shade now sways through the silent copse
To greet the ghosts of heroes, the bleeding heads;
And softly the dark flutes of autumn sound in the reeds.
O prouder grief! You brazen altars,
Today a great pain feeds the hot flame of the spirit,
The grandsons yet unborn.

        Georg Trakl translated by Michael Hamburger

Dulce et Decorum Est

Bent double, like old beggars under sacks,
Knock-kneed, coughing like hags, we cursed through sludge,
Till on the haunting flares we turned our backs
And towards our distant rest began to trudge.
Men marched asleep. Many had lost their boots
But limped on, blood-shod. All went lame; all blind;
Drunk with fatigue; deaf even to the hoots
Of tired, outstripped Five-Nines that dropped behind.

Gas! GAS! Quick, boys! An ecstasy of fumbling,
Fitting the clumsy helmets just in time;
But someone still was yelling out and stumbling
And flound'ring like a man in fire or lime . . .
Dim, through the misty panes and thick green light,
As under a green sea, I saw him drowning.

In all my dreams, before my helpless sight,
He plunges at me, guttering, choking, drowning.

If in some smothering dreams you too could pace
Behind the wagon that we flung him in,
And watch the white eyes writhing in his face,
His hanging face, like a devil's sick of sin;
If you could hear, at every jolt, the blood
Come gargling from the froth-corrupted lungs,
Obscene as cancer, bitter as the cud
Of vile, incurable sores on innocent tongues,
My friend, you would not tell with such high zest
To children ardent for some desperate glory,
The old lie: Dulce et decorum est.
Pro patria mori.

                                              Wilfred Owen

Through the Misty Panes by Richard Savage and Marian Savill

The Germans released about 68,000 tons of poison gas during the war, and the British and French released 51,000 tons. In total, 1,200,000 soldiers on both sides were gassed, of which 91,198 died. The German army gave much serious study to the development of chemical weapons and were the first to use it on a large scale. Three of the primary gases used in the war were chlorine, phosgene and mustard gas. Death by gas was often slow and painful. For example, a fatal dose of phosgene led to shallow breathing, retching, a raised pulse, an ashen face and the discharge of copious amounts of yellow liquid from the lungs. The effects of chlorine gas were also severe. Within a matter of seconds of inhaling the vapour it destroyed the victim's respiratory organs, bringing on violent choking attacks. Mustard gas was extremely powerful, causing internal and external blisters, essentially chemical burns. Many soldiers exposed to gas during the war suffered lifelong health problems; respiratory disease and failing eyesight were very common and their risk of cancer was much increased.

The One Eyed Man is King by Richard Savage

Advance into the Mist by Richard Savage

RS A number of my illustrations in this book use a technique called line and wash. I first draw the image in soft pencil then ink in the lines before applying thin washes of watercolour in tones of sepia, usually burnt senna and burnt umber. I like the way it gives the image an aged feel.

RS When I think of tanks, I remember family trips to Bovington Tank Museum as a child. The significance of these huge hunks of metal was wasted on me at the time. My uncle, commander of a bridging tank, was awarded the Military Medal in World War Two, for an act of heroism. Under fire, he was ordered to retreat, but remained in place to save the lives of his comrades. We hear snippets from our own family histories and we see them as matter of fact, we really don't see them as part of the grim tapestry of a global conflict. He was simply my Uncle Harry, and the significance of medals really had little or no impact on me until recently. The passing of my father and my three uncles, who all served in the Second World War, have given me the time to reflect more deeply on the human cost of war.

The development of tanks in World War One was as a response to the stalemate of trench warfare on the Western Front. An initial vehicle, nicknamed Little Willie, was constructed in Great Britain, at William Foster & Co, during August and September 1915. The prototype of a new design that would become the Mark I tank was demonstrated to the British Army on February 2, 1916. Although initially termed  *land ships* by the Landships Committee, production vehicles were named tanks to preserve secrecy. The term was chosen when it became known that the factory workers at William Foster referred to the first prototype as *the tank* because of its resemblance to a steel water tank.

 While the British took the lead in tank development, the French were not far behind, fielding their first tanks in April 1917 and going on to produce more tanks than all the other combatants combined. The Germans, on the other hand, were slower to develop tanks, concentrating on anti-tank weapons to use against British and French tanks, and producing only 20 of their *Moving Fortress,* seen right.

The first tanks were highly mechanically unreliable and very slow, not exceeding four miles an hour. There were problems that caused considerable attrition rates during combat, deployment and transit.

The heavily shelled terrain was impassable to conventional vehicles and only highly mobile tanks such as the Mark I and FTs performed reasonably well. The Mark I's rhomboid shape, caterpillar tracks, and 26 feet length meant that it could navigate obstacles, especially wide trenches, that wheeled vehicles could not. Crews gave their tanks endearing nicknames, like *Fray Bentos*, because they felt squashed like meat inside a tin can and a direct hit would turn the tank into a pressure cooker.

Several tanks sank into the soft Belgian mud and remain there to this day.

The Tsar Tank, seen right, or Lebedenko Tank was an unusual Russian armoured vehicle developed by Nikolai Lebedenko, Nikolai Zhukovsky, Boris Stechkin and Alexander Mikulin from 1914 onwards. The project was scrapped after initial tests deemed the vehicle to be underpowered and vulnerable to artillery fire.

The design differs from almost every other tank as it does not use caterpillar tracks but a tricycle design instead. The two front spoked wheels were nearly 27 feet in diameter; the back wheel was smaller, only 5 feet high and triple wheeled to ensure a high level of maneuverability. The upper cannon turret reached nearly 26 feet high, the hull was 39 feet wide with two more cannons in the sponsons. Additional weapons were also planned under the belly. Each wheel was powered by a 250 hp Sunbeam engine.

The huge wheels were intended to cross significant obstacles. However, due to miscalculations of the weight, the back wheel was prone to getting stuck in soft ground and ditches, and the front wheels were sometimes insufficient to pull it out. This led to a fiasco of tests before the high commission in August 1915. The tank remained in the location where it was tested, some 37 miles from Moscow until 1923 when it was finally taken apart for scrap.

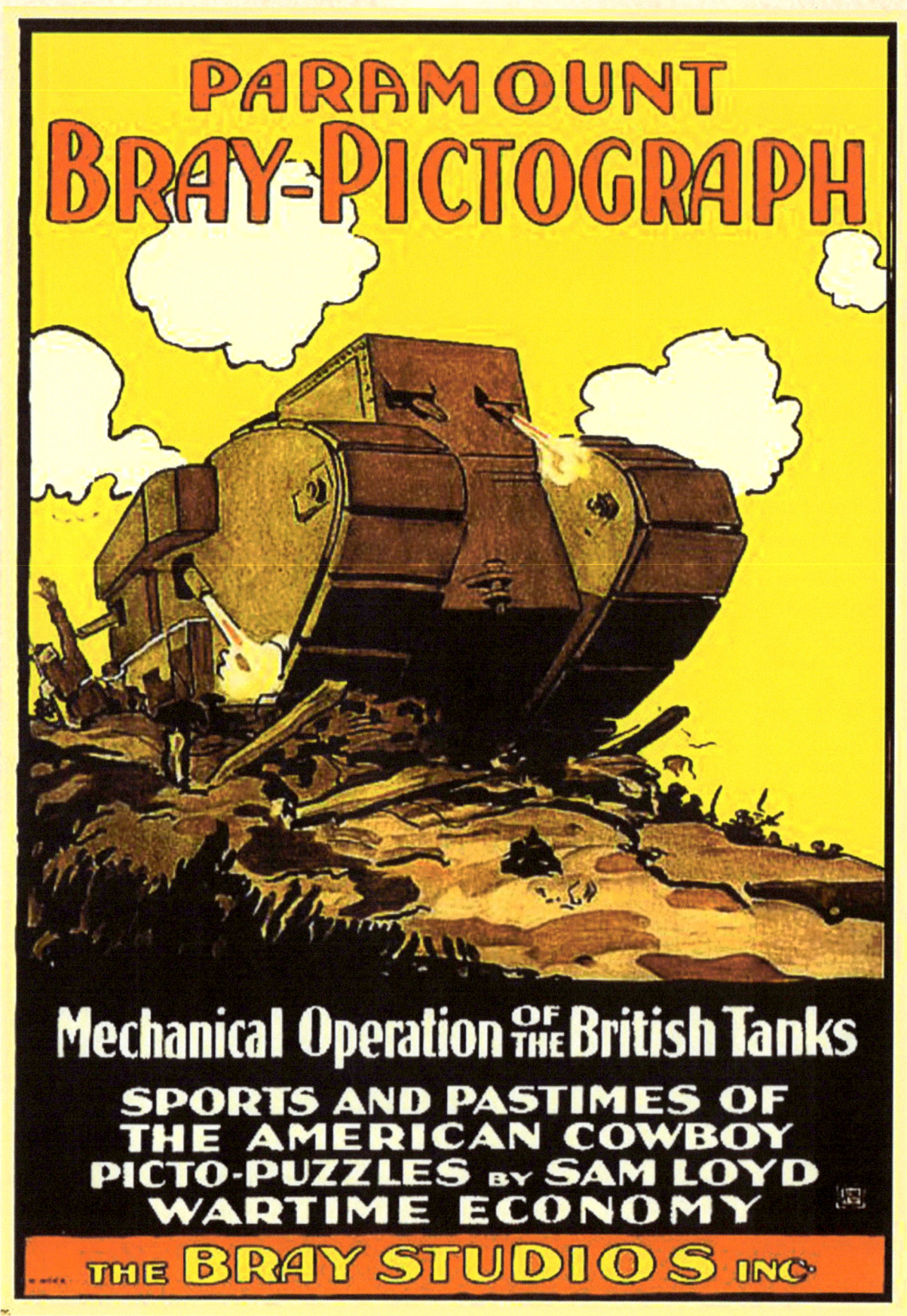

Through Mud and Blood to the Green Fields Beyond
by Richard Savage and Marian Savill

British Field Marshal, Lord Kitchener, whilst overseeing the trials of the tank, remarked that they were *a pretty mechanical toy but very limited military value.*

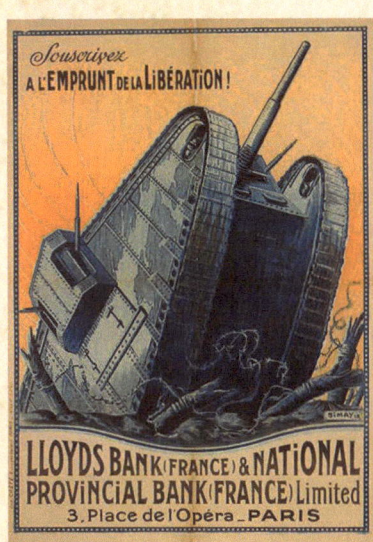

RS Examples of *splatter masks* worn by tank crews in an effort to protect the occupants from shrapnel injuries. I was drawn to these artefacts for their anachronistic Medieval look offering a solution to a 20th century problem.

In the research for our artwork we found many curious items. The acoustic mirror, seen right, initially made us laugh with it's absurd look but, after further research into this intriguing subject, it made sense.

The device concentrated sound waves. They were used to detect troop movements and artillery, and were a major area of research as an anti-aircraft early warning device before the introduction of radar.

The acoustic mirror programme, led by Dr William Sansome Tucker, gave Britain the methodology to use interconnected stations to pinpoint the position of an enemy in the sky. The system they developed for linking the stations and plotting aircraft movements was given to the early radar team. Acoustic mirrors and larger megaphone-like machines, odd as they looked, were used to locate the object with some degree of accuracy.

Large sound mirrors can still be seen in various places around the English coast; top left, Orford Ness, Suffolk, top right, Denge, Kent, bottom left, Abbots Cliff, Kent, bottom right, Hythe, Kent.

An assortment of strange looking acoustic mirrors; French, German and English.

Two other curious and unusual items we encountered during our research were, a rifle extension, seen above, which allowed troops to shoot over the top of a trench using a periscope to aim and a German bear trap, seen left. Both sides used similar devices in no man's land to hamper the advance of troops. These traps and other artefacts for the same purpose are still sometimes found in the ground today.

In response to growing casualties, the government introduced conscription in 1916. There was however a *conscience clause* which freed men from compulsory military service. There were several types of conscientious objector, some were pacifists, some political objectors who did not think of Germany as their enemy and there were religious objectors such as Quakers and Jehovah Witnesses.

Some objectors were still keen to *do their bit* though. They worked in weapons factories and some went to the trenches becoming stretcher bearers and taking other medical roles. There were others who refused to do anything for the war effort and these were known as *absolutists*.

Alledgedly the origins of the white feather as an icon of cowardice came from the world of cockfighting. It was thought that a cockerel sporting a white feather in its tail was a poor fighter. In 1914, Admiral Charles Fitzgerald founded the Order of the White Feather. The aim of the organisation was to encourage women to present white feathers to men not wearing a uniform and shame them into joining the army.

The campaign was so effective it spread to other nations in the Empire. It caused problems for the government as public servants were put under pressure to enlist. This prompted the Home Secretary to issue employees in state industries with badges reading *King and Country* to show they were serving the war effort. In the same way, *The Silver War Badge,* seen left, was given to service personnel who had been honourably discharged due to wounds or illness, to save them from being presented with white feathers. We came across many accounts of men being unfairly given white feathers. One of the more ironic accounts, was of Seaman George McKenzie Samson, of HMS River Clyde. Dressed in civilian clothes, he was presented with a white feather on his way to receive the Victoria Cross for gallantry in the Gallipoli campaign.

At the beginning of the war the Allies weren't prepared for the very high volume of casualties. The early medical care on the front in Flanders illustrates the great dedication of people, driven by their personal commitment. As increasing numbers of casualties passed through the medical system, care improved and became much more efficient. A complex system was set up rapidly for the treatment of wounded and sick soldiers which processed the casualty from the front line back to hospitals in England or, if deemed fit, back to their unit.

The first point of medical contact for a casualty would most likely have been an *aid post*, close behind the front line, where a Medical Officer, orderlies and stretcher bearers would have been based. The *Field Ambulance*, a mobile medical unit not a vehicle as suggested by the name, would provide relays of stretcher bearers and men skilled in first aid at *bearer posts* along the route of evacuation from the trenches. The Field Ambulances provided *Advanced Dressing Stations* where a casualty could receive further treatment and be stabilised in order to be evacuated to a *Casualty Clearing Station*. Men who were ill or injured would also be sent to the Dressing Stations and, for many, returned to their unit after first aid or some primary care.

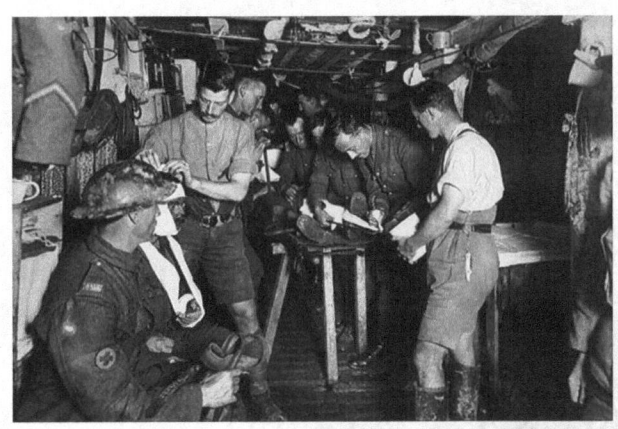

Advanced dressing station on Hill 60

Ideally, Dressing Stations, manned by the Royal Army Medical Corps, were set up in existing buildings, underground dug-outs and bunkers to afford them some protection from enemy shell fire and aerial attack. Once treated at a Dressing Station, casualties would be moved rearward a few miles to the Casualty Clearing Station. Depending on their injuries, men were sent on foot, or taken by horse drawn wagon, motor ambulance or light railway. The Hooge Chateau Advanced Dressing Station dealt with nearly 3500 casualties from the 1st to 14th August 1917, of which just under 1000 were on 10th and 11th August alone. These figures were not untypical for a unit involved in a major action.

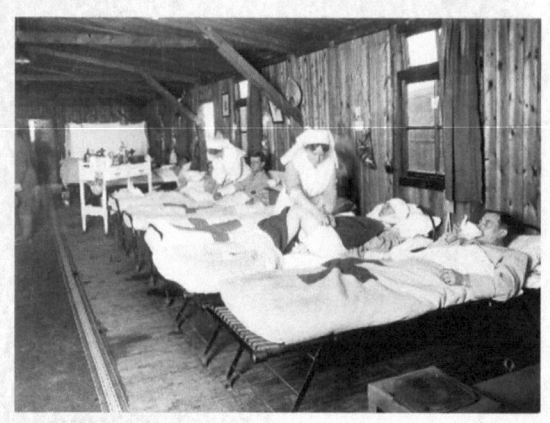

Australian Casualty Clearing Station

A Casualty Clearing Station, or CCS, was the first large, well-equipped and static medical facility that a wounded man would visit. Grouped in small clusters a few miles behind the lines and, where possible, close to a railway line, their role was to keep all serious cases that were unfit to travel any further, to treat and return lesser cases to their units and evacuate all others to *Base Hospitals*. A typical CCS could hold 1,000 men at any time and, at peak times of battle, would overflow with casualties. Serious operations such as limb amputations were carried out at the CCSs and some specialised in particular areas of treatment such as nervous disorders, skin diseases, infectious diseases and certain types of wounds. The serious nature of many wounds defied the medical facilities and skills of their staff and many CCS positions are today marked by large military cemeteries.

From the CCS, casualties advanced to *General Hospitals*, or directly to a port of embarkation if they had been identified as a *Blighty* case. In 1916, 734,000 wounded men were evacuated by train and another 17,000 by barge, on the Western Front alone. There were four ambulance trains in 1914 and twenty eight by July 1916.

Once admitted to a General Hospital, a soldier stood a reasonable chance of survival. More than half were evacuated from a General or Stationary Hospital for further treatment or convalescence in the United Kingdom. Stationary Hospitals, two per Division, could hold 400 casualties each and General Hospitals could hold 1040 patients. They were located near the army's principal bases at Boulogne, Le Havre, Rouen, Le Touquet and Etaples. The establishment of a General Hospital included 32 RAMC Medical Officers, 3 Chaplains, 73 female nurses and 206 RAMC troops acting as orderlies etc. The hospitals were enlarged in 1917 to as many as 2,500 beds.

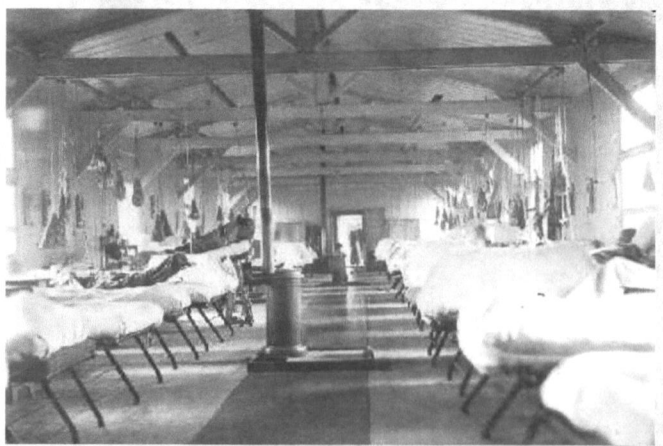

Base 10 Hospital Ward in LeTreport, France.

The Moribund Ward by Marian Savill

MS Reading various accounts of war time experiences from the nursing and medical perspective I kept coming across the term *moribund ward* which, I discovered, was where men with no hope of recovery were sent to be cared for, often their only treatment being sedation as they waited for death. The moribund ward was also known as the *dying tent*. Moribund struck me as such a sad mournful word and I wanted to create a reflective assemblage piece in remembrance of these dreadfully wounded, dying men. As I made The Moribund Ward a line from the Wilfred Owen poem, *But I Was Looking at the Permanent Stars*, came to mind; *The shadow of the morrow weighed on men*. Medical staff working in these wards must have found the work extremely harrowing. In 1917, the term moribund ward was dropped and replaced by resuscitation ward.

The war was the first test of the fledgling Army nursing services of Australia and New Zealand; the Australian Army Nursing Service (AANS) and the New Zealand Army Nursing Service (NZANS). The war brought a surge of volunteers among trained nurses keen to serve their country. The waiting lists were so long for overseas postings that at least 130 nurses chose to sail to England to join Queen Alexandra's Imperial Army Nursing Service. The first draft left Australia in September 1914. The Nursing Service served wherever Australian troops were sent including places such as Burma, India, the Persian Gulf, Egypt, Greece, Italy, France and England.

Founded in 1909, The Voluntary Aid Detachment, VAD, was an organisation providing field nursing services, here and in countries of the British Empire. Largely women and girls, VADs, were often from the middle and upper classes and unused to discipline and hardship. The military authorities were initially reluctant to accept them for overseas duty in hospitals but as the war progressed and VADs improved their skills and efficiency they became a vital part of the medical system. They not only worked in hospitals but also as ambulance drivers and cooks and many were decorated for distinguished service.

Edith Cavell was born in 1865 in Swardeston, near Norwich. In 1907, she was recruited as matron of a newly established nursing school, L'École Belge d'Infirmières Diplômées, in Brussels. By 1911, she was a training nurse for 3 hospitals, 24 schools and 13 kindergartens in Belgium.

In November 1914, after the German occupation of Brussels, Cavell began sheltering British soldiers and smuggling them into neutral Holland. This placed Cavell in direct violation of German military law. German authorities became suspicious and she was arrested on 3 August 1915 and charged with harbouring Allied soldiers. She was held in St Gilles prison for 10 weeks. She made three depositions to the German police, admitting that she had been responsible for the escape of about 60 British and 15 French soldiers and about 100 French and Belgians civilians of military age. The sentence according to German military law was death. The British government said they could do nothing to help her. Sir Horace Rowland of the Foreign Office said, *I am afraid that it is likely to go hard with Miss Cavell; I am afraid we are powerless.* Lord Robert Cecil, Under-Secretary for Foreign Affairs, said, *Any representation by us will do her more harm than good.*

The death sentence was carried out on 12 October 1915.

Jane Bemrose was born in Asterby, Lincolnshire. In 1915, Jane volunteered for war service. She joined the St John Ambulance Brigade and was sent to France.

On the night of 31st May 1918, she was working in a field hospital at Etaples when the hospital came under heavy enemy shelling. During the attack, Jane showed complete disregard for her own safety and rather than choosing cover she treated the wounded during three enemy bombardments. She was mentioned in despatches and subsequently awarded the Military Medal for Gallantry. She continued her work in France right up until the end of the war. Back in England, Jane continued her lifelong work as a nurse until retirement. She passed away in 1968 aged 86.

RS Something which has had a large influence on me for quite a large part of my life is a dark sense of humour, it is slightly sarcastic, slightly anarchic. It helps me to deal with the most appalling of circumstances and helps articulate feelings and vent emotions in a way like no other. The old expression *I didn't know whether to laugh or cry* comes to mind. Many films and TV shows have used off beat comedy, examples of which would be the fourth series of *Blackadder* and the film, *Wipers Times*. I remember watching *Oh, What a Lovely War!* with my father in the early seventies, I was a little too young to appreciate the nuances of the humour at the time, but I have watched the film many times since and it led me to find out a little of it's origins.

Oh! What a Lovely War, a 1969 musical film directed by Richard Attenborough, was originally based on the radio musical, The Long Long Trail by Charles Chilton, first aired on the BBC Home Service in 1962, telling the story of the First World War through the songs sung by soldiers. Gerry Raffles heard the second broadcast, and developed the idea into a stage musical The musical premiered at the Theatre Royal, Stratford East on 19 March 1963.

So, it came as no surprise to find original source material from the troops in the trenches with their own form of gallows humour.

Hildern V.A.D.
28.1.1918

All the Worlds a Stage,
And Men, and Women, Merely Players,
They have their Exits, and their Entrances,
And one Man, in his Time, Plays many Parts.
"As you like it"
And.
"This", is the Hardest, Part I have ever Played.

Marc. C. Challands.
1st Dorset Reg:

Wounded at
"Passchendale"
Dec. 1917.

The Wipers Times was a trench newspaper produced between early February 1916 and February 1918 by British soldiers from the 12th Battalion Sherwood Foresters in France.

Early in 1916, stationed in the front line at Ypres some 12th Battalion soldiers discovered an abandoned printing press. A sergeant, who had been a printer in civilian life, salvaged it and printed a sample page. Wipers was soldier slang for Ypres and so the The Wipers Times began.

A lot of the staff involved in the paper are not known, but the editor was Captain, later Lieutenant-Colonel, F. J. Roberts and the sub-editor was Lieutenant F. H. Pearson. A notable contributor to the paper was Artilleryman Gilbert Frankau, a popular British novelist. Another contributor, E.J. Couzens, drew a portrait of a chinless platoon commander, with a cane, wondering *Am I as offensive as I might be?* This became the paper's motif.

The newspaper included verse, reflections, wry in-jokes, mock adverts and parodies of the military situation. It had a dark, humorously ironic style that can be seen in modern day satirical magazines such as Private Eye.

WIPERS & DISTRICT GAS COMPANY.
—o—o—o—
ISSUE OF NEW STOCK.
—o—o—o—

Owing to the ever-increasing use of Gas in the neighbourhood of Wipers, the Company are increasing their plant to cope with the extra demand. They hope to be able to supply all (and more) than the consumers want.

The Company has Branch Offices at any Artillery Headquarters, where further information can be obtained.

Stock will be issued at 18*l* and 60*l*.

Rapid and regular delivery guaranteed.
WIPERS & DISTRICT GAS COY.
R. A. GUNNER, Secretary.

The world wasn't made in a day,
And Eve didn't ride on a bus,
But most of the world's in a sandbag,
The rest of its plastered on us.

"DEAD COW FARM" CINEMA
THIS WEEK—SPECIAL PROGRAMME.

"PIPPED ON THE PARAPET."
THIS EXCITING TALE HAS BEEN FILMED AT ENORMOUS EXPENSE, FEATURING THE CELEBRATED SCOTCH COMEDIAN,
MAC KENSEN.
—o—o—o—o—
OTHER ITEMS.
—o—o—o—o—
"OVER THE TOP."
A SCREAMING FARCE.
—o—o—o—o—
"THE EMPTY JAR."
A RUM TRAGEDY
—o—o—o—o—
PRICES AS USUAL.   OPEN ALWAYS.

THE B.E.F. TIMES.

WITH WHICH ARE INCORPORATED

The Wipers Times, The "New Church" Times, The Kemmel Times & The Somme-Times.

| No 4. Vol 1 | Monday, March 5th, 1917 | Price 1 Franc. |

THE FOSSE THEATRE OF VARIETIES.

This Week—Special Engagement.

THE MAUDE TROUPE
IN THEIR SCREAMING FARCE,
WHAT'S THE BAG, DAD?
FEATURING ENVER IN HIS LITTLE SONG
"I'M ALL DRESSED UP AND NOWHERE TO GO."

FILM PLAYS.

COMEDY—"WILLIE'S TURKEY."
IN THREE PARTS
Topical—"LETTING GO THE ANCHOR."
BY HIND AND BERG FILM PLAY SYNDICATE.

PRICES AS USUAL   BOOK EARLY.

Cloth Hall.
Ypres.

Great Attraction This Week
Messrs. INFANTRY, ARTILLERY & Co.
Present their Screamingly Funny Farce,
Entitled:

"BLUFF"

THIS FARCE PROMISES TO BE A GREAT SUCCESS AND A LONG RUN IS EXPECTED

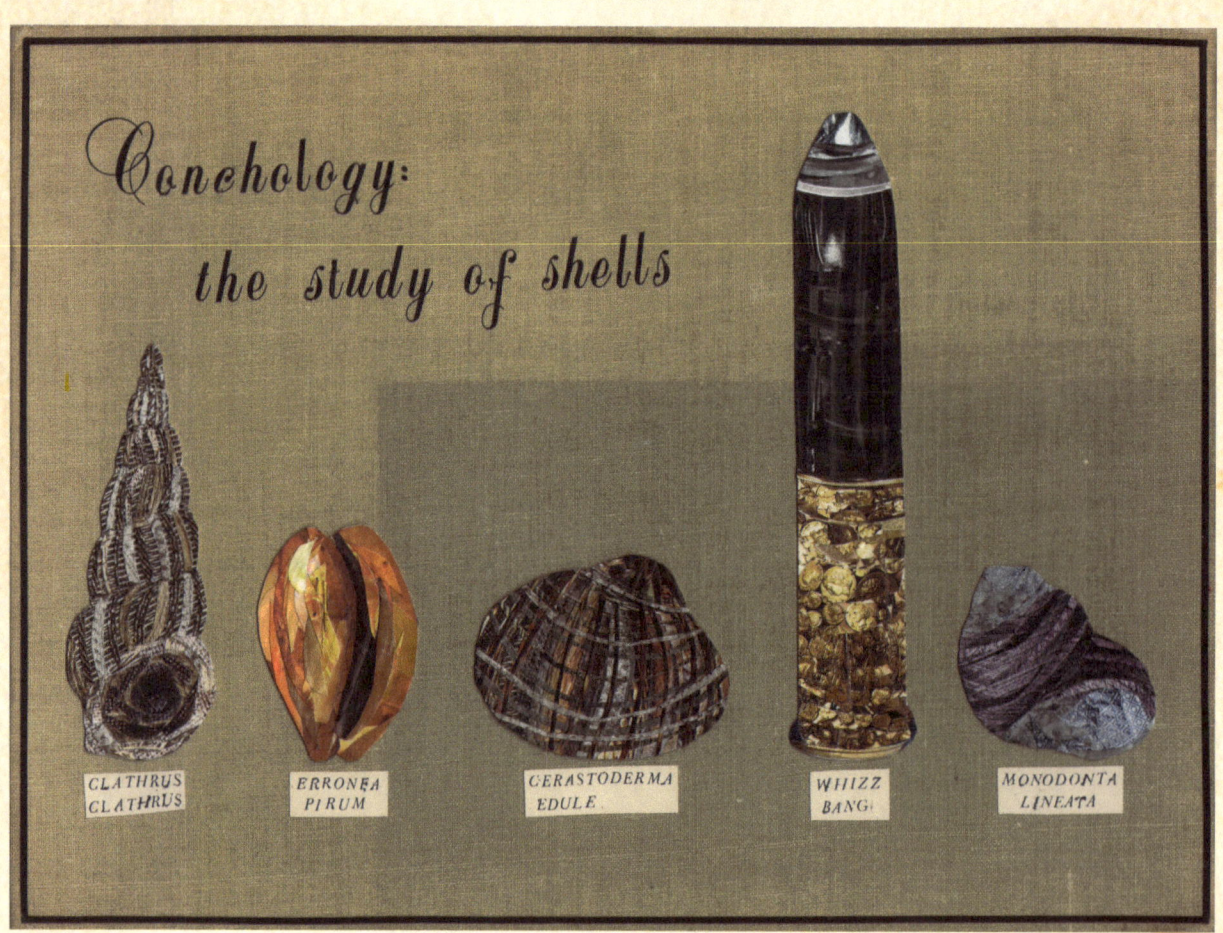

Conchology by Marian Savill

MS In the spirit of The Wipers Times, a satirical piece of collage suggested itself to me. Created predominantly from magazine pages, a whizz bang shell sits among seashells in a homespun classification setting. A *whizz bang* was a 7.7cm German artillery shell so named, by the troops, because of the sound they made in flight and on explosion.

A Christmas card from the trenches

In 1914, the seventeen year old Princess Mary, seen below, launched a campaign to raise funds to send every man in uniform a gift from the nation on Christmas Day. The response from the public was overwhelming and the decision was made to make embossed brass tin boxes filled with useful items. The contents varied but could include a pipe, tobacco, cigarettes, sweets, chocolate, pencil, a Christmas card and a picture of the princess. The campaign was so successful that by the time it was wound up in 1920 it had raised almost £200,000 and provided over two and a half million boxes.

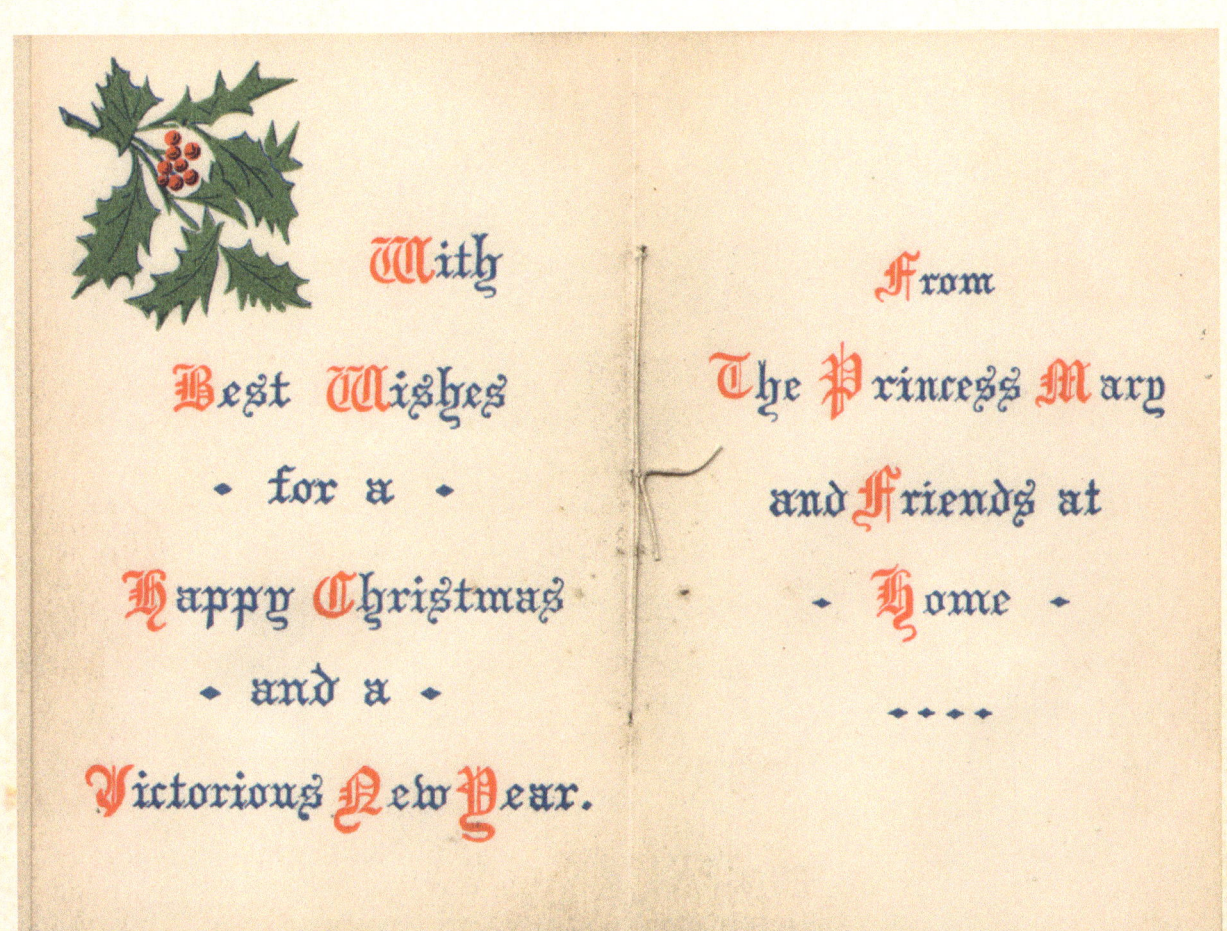

MS As a huge fan of traditional correspondence, I was very curious to find out about the handling of post during the war.

To my mind, one of the British army's most effective weapons during the war was being able to keep the morale of the troops high and contact with loved ones was vital in this. Letters and parcels from home helped keep boredom at bay, distract men from the horrors of war and afford them much comfort.

In December 1914, a new sorting office, the London Home Depot, seen below, was built in Regents Park to deal with the volume of mail for the Western Front. Covering five acres, it was, at that time, the largest wooden building in the world. Every week 12.5 million letters left Home Depot bound for the front and it took just two days for them to arrive at their destination. Over the course of the war, the Home Depot processed 2 billion letters and 114 million parcels.

Mail bags were transported to ports by train or lorry and then by ship across the English Channel. In France, the Army Postal Service (APS) had depots in Boulogne, Calais and Le Havre where mail was received and then moved forward by train and lorry again. Postal orderlies would then sort the mail by the roadside and deliver to the front by cart, aiming for it to arrive with the evening meal.

MS Silk embroidered postcards were extremely popular during the war. British and American soldiers particularly liked sending these souvenirs home to loved ones. French and Belgian women were employed to hand embroider the complex designs onto rolls of silk organdie which were then sent to Paris factories for mass cutting and mounting on card. Some designs were made of two pieces of silk to form an envelope which contained a message card or handkerchief. It's estimated that ten million silk postcards were made during the war providing much needed income for many French women. All the cards seen here were sent home from the Western Front by my husband's grandfather and great uncles, all of whom miraculously survived the war.

Looking at the subject of the 1914 Christmas truce was interesting as neither of us are at all interested in football. However it was such an iconic event we just knew we had to explore the subject further.

On Christmas Eve, the weather had changed to a hard frost, ironically this had made trench conditions a little more bearable. It had been a difficult day and records show that 98 British soldiers died, many were victims of sniper fire. During the afternoon and early evening, British infantry were astonished to see many decorated Christmas trees on enemy parapets. Accounts of the time tell of singing of carols, hymns and popular songs, and a gradual exchange of communication and even meetings in some areas. Many of these meetings were to arrange collection of bodies. The tension reduced to the point that individuals would walk across no man's land to talk to their adversaries. Seen below, Saxon Regiment and Royal Warwickshire Regiment soldiers meeting in no man's land. There is plenty of evidence that soccer was played that Christmas Day, in some cases between  men of the same nationality but, in several places, between troops from the opposing armies. Some are documented; a letter written by a doctor attached to the Rifle Brigade, published in The Times on 1 January 1915, reported *A football match... played between them and us in front of the trench.* Other accounts are more specific; games played between teams of opposing armies include that of the German 133rd Royal Saxon Regiment against Scottish troops and Argyll and the Sutherland Highlanders against German troops.

The truce is often seen as a symbolic moment of peace and humanity amidst one of the most violent events of human history. It was not ubiquitous; in parts of the front, fighting continued throughout Christmas Day, while in others, little more than an arrangement to recover bodies was made. In 1915, a few units again arranged ceasefires with their opponents over Christmas, but it was not nearly as widespread as in 1914; this was due, in part, to strongly worded orders from the high commands of both sides prohibiting such fraternisation. In 1916, after the bloody battles of the Somme and Verdun, and the start of widespread poison gas use, soldiers on both sides increasingly viewed the other side as less than human, and no more Christmas truces were sought.

A Fair Kick of the Ball by Richard Savage and Marian Savill

Our kinetic pictures are created using heavy body acyclic on canvas. Our joint work evolves slowly, each piece is built up over time; it can take weeks and, in some cases, months for the picture to form. Yet the way the art is created is spontaneous and full of movement. When we are painting, we move around the canvas, two individuals but painting together, our thin ribbons of paint crossing as the layers build. We have both been delighted with the reaction the work has provoked; so many people have wanted to touch them as the texture is so rich.

With the outbreak of war and Kitchener's call for a hundred thousand volunteers, Scottish football did not hang back. Almost all clubs saw players leave to go to war immediately. Sir George McCrae approached the Heart of Midlothian players concerning a new battalion he was forming. Thirteen of the players were persuaded by his arguments to enlist in the 16th Royal Scots. The news of their enlistment brought several hundred Hearts fans, university students, and players from other clubs, such as Raith Rovers, Falkirk, Dunfermline and Hibernian, to the battalion. Mossend Burnvale, aka *The Cow-Punchers,* also joined. About thirty Heart of Midlothian men had enlisted in total. Of the original thirteen, seven did not return and the majority of those who did, suffered physical or mental wounds.

Hearts at the Somme 1916

No Man's Game by Richard Savage

Second Lieutenant Walter Tull was born on 28th April 1888 and brought up in an orphanage in Bethnal Green, London, along with his brother, following the death of their parents. His grandmother was a slave in Barbados

Tull was a professional English footballer who played for Tottenham Hotspur and then moved to Northampton Town, where he made 111 first team appearances. He was the second person of Afro-Caribbean descent to play in the top division of the Football League. His professional football career began after he was spotted whilst playing for his local amateur club, Clapton FC. He began playing for Clapton FC in 1908 and within a few months he had won winners' medals in the FA Amateur Cup, London County Amateur Cup and London Senior Cup. In March 1909, the *Football Star* called him *the catch of the season*.

During the First World War, Tull served in the Footballers' Battalion of the Middlesex Regiment, and fought in the Battle of the Somme in 1916. He was the first Afro-Caribbean to be commissioned as an infantry officer in the British Army. He was commissioned as a Second Lieutenant on 30 May 1917 despite the 1914 Manual of Military Law specifically excluding *Negroes* and *Mulattos* from exercising command as officers.

Tull fought in Italy in 1917–18, and was mentioned in despatches for *gallantry and coolness* while leading his company of 26 men on a raiding party into enemy territory. He returned to France in 1918, and was killed in action on 25 March during the Spring Offensive; his body was never recovered.

Campaigners have called for a statue to be erected in his honour, and Northampton South MP, Brian Binley, has campaigned for Tull to be posthumously awarded the Military Cross.

The US policy, when the war began, was one of neutrality although they did supply arms to the Allied powers. The great majority of American civilians were in favour of remaining neutral, although at the outbreak of war thousands of US citizens tried to enlist in the German army.

As the war continued, opinion slowly became more divided, partly in response to German war atrocities in Belgium. In 1915, German U-boat, U20, sank the British liner, Lusitania. Of the 1,959 passengers and crew 1,195 lost their lives. Among those lost were 128 of the 139 Americans citizens aboard. President Woodrow Wilson said, *America is too proud to fight*, effectively agreeing to remain neutral if German U-boats did not attack American shipping.

Many in positions of power in the American government argued it was better to put domestic self interest first. It was also argued that America's armed forces at the time were not substantial enough for war, so a policy of training additional men was started which doubled America's armed forces.

The German Foreign Minister started talks with the Mexican government, offering them money to help them recover Texas, New Mexico and Arizona, Mexico territories they had lost during the Mexican–American War 70 years earlier. British intelligence intercepted messages between Germany and Mexico and passed them to Washington.

Germany resumed unrestricted submarine warfare in January 1917. U-boats continued to sink US merchant ships and the United States formally entered the war from April 6, 1917.

The US government started a campaign of domestic propaganda to win over the minds of a war sceptic nation. Tens of thousands of government-selected community leaders gave brief carefully scripted pro-war speeches at thousands of public gatherings. Other forms of propaganda included newsreels, photos, magazine and newspaper articles, and billboards. The Boy Scouts of America distributed war pamphlets and helped sell war bonds.

Arriving at the rate of 10,000 a day, the effect of US forces on the battlefields of France was immense. Fresh American troops were enthusiastically greeted by the war-weary Allied armies in the summer of 1918.

Not all American offensives were effective, as many American commanders used the flawed tactics that Allied troops had abandoned early in the war. The addition of US soldiers gave the allies a decisive edge. German morale had collapsed on the western and home fronts and the war came to an end.

During the war, the US mobilised over 4,000,000 military personnel and suffered 110,000 deaths including 43,000 due to the 1918 influenza pandemic. The war saw a dramatic expansion of the US government and a significant increase in the size of the US military forces, in an effort to harness the war effort.

RS My fascination of military aviation comes from a combination of reading Boy's Own books and comics, leading on to historical fiction and non-fiction, and listening to my father's enthusiasm on all things military; he was a Royal Marine in the Second World War and very well read on military history. He encouraged trips to museums and galleries. I well remember frequent trips to the Imperial War Museums in London and Duxford as well as the Royal Air Force Museum in Hendon, where my father, incidentally, was contracts manager for the Battle of Britain section. We also made regular trips to the Shuttleworth Collection. My father made a great tour guide and I never failed to be amazed at the depth of his knowledge. I also have a keen interest in films, particularly aviation films. Films that further inspired this section of the book are, Von Richthofen and Brown, Aces High and The Blue Max. As a boy it was the daring do that caught my imagination. As an adult, my obsession matured into a deep regard for the brave young men that took to the air in wooden frames covered with stretched canvas and the cost to those young men.

The Only Pup by Richard Savage

 Guy Ellis was studying for his Civil Service exam when, in 1915, he joined up, aged seventeen. In April 1916, Guy volunteered for The Royal Flying Corps. He was commissioned in January 1917 and posted to 57 Squadron, near Ypres. In July 1917, a new offensive at Ypres was planned. On 11th July, some two weeks before the battle began, an allied air offensive involving 700 aircraft began. The following day one of these aircraft flew with Guy as observer. It is not documented what brought down the plane, ending his life, aged nineteen.

For me, the story of Guy Ellis highlights the pitifully short life expectancy of anyone serving in a front line squadron and both sides of the conflict were subject to the same short odds of survival. It also brings up the subject of bailing out and the fact that aircrew were not issued with parachutes. The official view at the time was *possession of a parachute might impair a pilot's nerve when in difficulties so that he would make improper use of his parachute.* If the plane was on fire or too damaged to fly or land, it left the crew few options; to sit in and wait for the inevitable, to jump, or to save a last shot for themselves.

Aviation at this time was in its infancy and flying was a hazardous business. In April 1917, the worst month for the entire war, the average life expectancy of a British pilot on the Western Front was just 93 flying hours. More men were killed in training than in combat. Observation balloons had been used in several wars, utilised extensively for artillery spotting. Germany employed Zeppelins for reconnaissance and for strategic bombing raids. Aeroplanes were just coming into military use at the outset of the war. Britain was slow to start and initially relied largely on the French aircraft industry, especially for their aircraft engines.

In August 1914, of approximately 184 allied aircraft, Britain contributed three squadrons with about thirty serviceable machines. Pilots and engineers learned from experience, leading to the development of many specialised types, including fighters, bombers, and ground attack-aeroplanes. One function of the squadrons was photographic reconnaissance. Glass plate cameras helped to build a complete mosaic map of the enemy trench system.

On Christmas Eve, 1914, a German aircraft dropped a bomb on Dover: the first air raid in British history. An average 1914 plane could only carry very small bomb loads. The bombs, and their storage, were still very elementary, and effective bomb sights were yet to be developed but, the beginnings of strategic and tactical bombing date from the earliest days of the war. Initially, air combat was extremely rare, and definitely subordinate to reconnaissance but it soon progressed to throwing grenades and other objects, even grappling hooks. The first aircraft brought down by another was an Austrian reconnaissance aircraft rammed in September 1914 by Russian pilot, Pyotr Nesterov. Both planes crashed, killing all occupants. Pilots began firing pistols and single shot rifles at enemy aircraft. In October 1914, French pilot, Louis Quenault, opened fire on a German aircraft with a machine gun for the first time. Airco DH.1, was a pusher type. These had the engine and propeller behind the pilot, facing backward. This

provided an optimal machine gun position from which the gun could be fired directly forward without an obstructing propeller. It made it easier to reload in flight. On traditional aircraft, machine guns could be mounted on the upper wing to fire over the propeller. The development of the interrupter gear later allowed the machine gun to fire through the propeller.

The lyrics from a song included in The RFC/RNAS Handbook 1914-18 by Peter Cooksley:

It's the only way

If by some delightful chance,
When you're flying out in France,
Some Bosche machine you meet,
Very slow and obsolete,
Don't turn round to watch your tail,
Tricks like that are getting stale;
Just put down you beastly nose,
And murmur, "Chaps, here goes!"

It's the only, only way,
It's the only trick to play;
He's the only Hun, you're the only Pup,
And he's only getting the wind right up,
So go on, and do not stop
Till his tail's damn near your prop,
If he only crashes this side in flames,
Well, you'll only know they'll believe your claims—
So keep him right
In the Aldis sight
It's the o-o-only way!

If on escort you should go
When the "Fees" are very slow,
While the Archies grumph and roar,
And Huns gather by the score;
If a nasty Hun should strive,
There's no choice at all, and so
Down your nose must go!

I hate to shoot a Hun down without him seeing me, for although this method is in accordance with my doctrine, it is against what little sporting instincts I have left.
James McCudden, VC, RFC, 1917

Captain Arthur Roy Brown, DSC and bar RNAS, was a Canadian flying ace. The Royal Air Force officially credited Brown with shooting down Manfred von Richthofen, the *Red Baron*, although it is probably unlikely that Brown fired the bullet that caused Richthofen's death. What is less well known is that Brown never lost a pilot in his flight during combat, a rare accolade for an air unit commander of the war. This was due largely to his demands for a *breaking in* period in which new pilots flew to the combat zone but didn't take part in the action in order to observe how the combat worked and how their planes handled.

Captain Roy Brown by Richard Savage

Since boyhood I have been fascinated by the characters of Roy Brown and Manfred Von Richthofen. I remember watching the film Von Richthofen and Brown, an account of the two pilots, and I became totally absorbed by the way the two men were portrayed. Of course, I have no way to be sure the portrayal was in any way accurate. I would like to share a fragment from the film; part of an interview with Brown. I have not been able to verify if the interview took place but it has lodged in my mind as summing up some of the thoughts and views of pilots at the time.

Reporter : Do you like France?

Brown : It's a nice country, many of my friends will be staying after the war.

Reporter : Are the German planes dangerous?

Brown : The Germans, they are dangerous. Their planes are dangerous too. They kill as many Germans as we do, in the same way our planes do us.

Manfred von Richthofen by Richard Savage

Manfred Albrecht Freiherr von Richthofen, widely known as the Red Baron, was a German fighter pilot with the Imperial German Army Air Service, *Luftstreitkräfte* He is considered the top air ace of the war, being officially credited with 80 air combat victories.

He started in the cavalry and transferred to the Air Service in 1915, becoming one of the first members of *Jasta* 2 in 1916. In 1917, he became leader of *Jagdgeschwader 1,* known as *The Flying Circus*. By 1918, he was regarded as a national hero in Germany, and well known amongst opposing forces.

I found some quotes I could directly attribute to Von Richthofen that I think say something about the man.

Of course, with the increasing number of aeroplanes one gains increased opportunities for shooting down one's enemies, but at the same time, the possibility of being shot down one's self increases.

Everything depends on whether we have for opponents those French tricksters or those daring rascals, the English. I prefer the English. Frequently their daring can only be described as stupidity. In their eyes it may be pluck and daring.

Fight on and fly on to the last drop of blood and the last drop of fuel, to the last beat of the heart.

Seen right, the famous bright red Fokker Triplain.

Richthofen was shot down and killed near Amiens on 21st April 1918, aged 26.

RS William Dring was an observer, flight engineer, photographer and gunner. I came across his photo album some twenty five years ago, as a friend of his daughter Kathy Ellis and her son, Ian. William enlisted in the RFC in March, 1917 at the age of 19.   As soon as we started the book, I just knew I would have to include material from his album as, for me, it's the embodiment of everyday people in extraordinary times. The album tells its stories through its pictures and brief poignant captions.

in working dress

Vickers Vimy ready to fly to Egypt crashed into side of hill in Italy caught fire pilot Major Darery (on left) burned to death observer Capt Darley trying to rescue his brother is disfigured for life

Above left, an aerial picture of an Ypres gas attack. Above right, a plane crash site. Seen left, William, in uniform.

Seen right, William, not long before his death in 1982 aged 84

Christopher Charles Hall

Remembrance by Marian Savill

MS My paternal grandfather, Christopher Charles Hall, was born in 1898 and enlisted in October 1916, initially serving with the Hampshire Cyclists, scooting about with empty sandbags on the back of his bike! Grandad never really spoke much about his war time experiences and my interest wasn't piqued until I started to research my family history at the age of 18. I voraciously read all manner of books about the war; firsthand accounts, military history, romanticised fiction, it was all absorbed. Although I was horrified at the descriptions of the trench conditions, hideous injuries and tales of loss, it remained words on the page until my grandfather talked about it and even then, as now, it remained incomprehensible to me. At the age of 18, the age I then was, he was in Belgium enduring the appalling conditions of the trenches fighting for his country.

Remembrance is an uncomplicated piece with a clear message; we should never forget those who fought for us. In my collage work, I love to use layers and I often print images on tissue paper, as with this piece, to create depth.

Grandad arrived in Boulogne in April 1918. He had one elder brother, Frank, who had joined the Royal Marines. When Grandad disembarked in France almost the first person he met was his brother, Frank. Neither knew the whereabouts of the other and their surprise and delight must have been huge.

Grandad was injured at Verdun in May 1918, shot in the left arm. The injury was bad enough for him to be sent home to England and he didn't return to the front. He recovered well, married in 1922 and lived a full and long life, dying in 1988 at the age of 89. Uncle Frank survived the war too, spending his working life as a train engine driver.

Frank Hall

Christopher Charles Hall, standing, far right third row, recuperating from his injury at Hampton Grange, Herefordshire

My husband's great uncle, Edward James Grist, served with the 19th Battalion London Regiment and was killed during the 3rd Battle of Ypres in August 1917. He is one of over 54,000 soldiers who died in the Ypres salient with no known grave and their names are commemorated on the Menin Gate war memorial in Belgium.

Edward James Grist

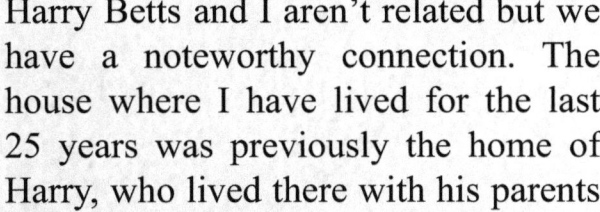

Harry Betts and I aren't related but we have a noteworthy connection. The house where I have lived for the last 25 years was previously the home of Harry, who lived there with his parents and eight siblings. Dubbed the *Unsung Hero of the Fens,* Harry joined up in September 1914 at the age of 18 and served with the Cambridgeshire Regiment. He transpired to be a very able soldier and at the age of 21 he became the youngest Company Sergeant Major in the British Army. He was courageously fearless and heroic and was awarded the MC, DCM & Bar for his many actions. Sadly, he was killed in action at the Battle of Bapaume in Ausust 1918 and is buried in Beacon Cemetery at Sailly-Laurette in France.

George William Burdett Clare VC was born in St Ives, Cambridgeshire but at an early age moved to Chatteris. He was a private in the 5th Lancers Royal Irish. He was awarded the Victoria Cross for his actions on 28th/29th November, 1917 at Bourlon Wood, France during the Battle of Cambrai, where he lost his life, aged 28. He has no known grave but is recorded on the Cambrai Memorial.

His citation read:
For most conspicuous bravery and devotion to duty when, acting as a stretcher-bearer, during a most intense and continuous enemy bombardment, Pte. Clare dressed and conducted wounded over the open to the dressing station about 500 yards away. At one period when all the garrison of a detached post, which was lying out in the open about 150 yards to the left of the line occupied, had become casualties, he crossed the intervening space, which was continually swept by heavy rifle and machine gun fire, and having dressed all the cases, manned the post single-handed till a relief could be sent. Pte. Clare then carried a seriously wounded man through intense fire to cover, and later succeeded in getting him to the dressing station. At the dressing station, he was told that the enemy was using gas shells to a large extent in the valley below, and as the wind was blowing the gas towards the line of trenches and shell holes occupied, he started on the right of the line and personally warned every company post of the danger, the whole time under shell and rifle fire. This very gallant soldier was subsequently killed by a shell.

RS In contrast to the well documented life of George Claire, Herbert Stacey, is relatively obscure. He enlisted in the Territorial Army and was later conscripted to the Machine Gun Corps. Looking up his service history gave me few facts about his time at war. You might ask, why include him? When we think about the anonymity of the Great War, it is easy to get caught up in the sheer scale of the conflict, I think it is crucial to remember that each person was an individual with their own story.

My connection with Herbert Stacey is a rather unusual one. He is not family, but I know his family well. Back in 1987, I bought a public house from his son.

Family histories and stories are funny things; rumour and myth build up over the years. It is interesting to put fact against fiction. Both of my grandfathers served in the war. I hadn't explored it further until a few years back and what I found was quite different from the family stories. None of the stories were malicious or intended to deceive, it is my belief the accounts changed in the telling, somewhat like Chinese whispers.

My mother's account of her father's war experience; John Perrin, born 1888, into a large family. He was conscripted into the Royal Kings Own Yorkshire Light Infantry. Once in France, he found trench warfare particularly hard, cold, wet and hungry but the troops just made the best of what they had. They endured bugs and lice in their clothing, they would get a lighted taper and burn the little creatures out of their puttees. He fought in the battle at Ypres, he lay badly wounded and prayed for stretcher bearers to find him. Eventually two did come along, took one look at him and said, *Blimey, mate, you've got a 'blighty' there*. Treated and eventually repatriated to England, he made a slow recovery to good health. The family history told of an account of the loss of five brothers, missing believed killed, at Passchendaele, the Dardanelles and the Somme. The reality differed in the respect that only one sibling, Eli, was actually killed in action in 1915 at Gallipoli, others were lost but largely through illness and not as a result of war. My grandfather died in 1962, the year I was born.

The Perrin family

My paternal grandfather gave the impression of being an old soldier, told stories of the war, gave every impression that he was in the thick of it. However, the research told a different story. It transpired he never left England. He was in the Territorial Army before the war, embodied for military service in August 1914, with the 1st Battalion Yorkshire & Lancashire Regiment. When the 1st battalion went to France, he stayed behind, posted into the 2nd, 3rd and 4th Battalion before eventually becoming attached to Messrs. Kaiser Engineering as a munitions worker. He effectively stayed in the army but worked in munitions until demobbed in January 1919. He most likely would have still worn uniform to show he was engaged in war work. We could find no reason for this as an anomaly of war but think it interesting. He could not have been the only case of this kind during the war.

The Gallipoli Campaign, also known as the Dardanelles Campaign, took place on the Gallipoli peninsula in the Ottoman Empire between 25th April 1915 and 9th January 1916. The peninsula forms the northern bank of the Dardanelles, a strait that provides a sea route to, what was then, the Russian Empire, one of the Allied powers during the war. Russia's allies, Britain and France, launched a naval attack, followed by an amphibious landing with the eventual aim of capturing the Ottoman capital of Constantinople, modern day Istanbul. The naval attack was repelled and, after eight months of fighting, with many casualties on both sides, the land campaign also failed and the invasion force was withdrawn to Egypt.

Gallipoli

Upon the margin of a rugged shore
There is a spot now barren, desolate,
A place of graves, sodden with human gore
That Time will hallow, Memory consecrate.

There lie the ashes of the mighty dead,
The youth who lit with flame Obscurity,
Fought true for Freedom, won thro' rain of lead
Undying fame, their immortality.

The stranger wand'ring when the war is over,
The ploughman there driving his coulter deep,
The husbandman who golden harvests reap-
From hill and ravine, from each plain and cover
Will hear a shout, see phantoms on the marge,
See men again making a deathless charge.

John William Streets

Towards Gallipoli by Marian Savill

MS I had just finished reading *To Hell and Back: The Banned Account of Gallipoli,* a narrative of the experiences of Australian soldier, Sydney Loch, which was banned when it was first published in 1916, and was inspired to create a collage piece on the subject. I used vintage book illustrations for the collage, building layers as I worked from the background to the foreground. I chose to work in monochrome, as opposed to the idyllic vivid blues usually associated with the Aegean Sea, to add dramatic impact. Suggestive of the view towards the coastline, showing only sea, cliffs and sky, for me, this abstract representation conjures up the apprehension of the thousands of men, seeing the cliffs for the first time as they arrived for the ill fated Gallipoli campaign.

More than 500,000 troops fought in the Gallipoli campaign. The fighting cost 58,000 Allied lives, including nearly 9000 Australians and nearly 3000 New Zealanders, with close to 200,000 more wounded and sick. The insanitary conditions caused enteric fever, dysentery and diarrhoea. It's estimated that 145,000 British soldiers fell ill during the campaign.

The battle was one of the greatest Ottoman victories during the war and a major Allied failure. In Turkey, it is regarded as a defining moment in the nation's history, a final surge in the defence of the motherland as the Ottoman Empire crumbled. The struggle formed the basis for the Turkish War of Independence and the founding of the Republic of Turkey eight years later under Mustafa Kemal Atatürk, who first rose to prominence as a commander at Gallipoli. The campaign is often considered as marking the birth of national consciousness in Australia and New Zealand and the date of the landing, 25 April, is known as *Anzac Day*. It remains the most significant commemoration of military casualties and veterans in those two countries, surpassing Armistice Day, 11th November.

On its way to the Dardanelles, to collect wounded soldiers, HMHS Britannic was sunk. A sad fact in itself, but it drew our attention to the fascinating story of Violet Jessop, who served for the Red Cross on the ship. Violet famously survived disasters on all three sister ships; Titanic, Olympic and Britannic.

In 1911, aged 23, Violet was serving as a stewardess on RMS Olympic, the largest civilian liner of the day. On 20th September, the Olympic collided with HMS Hawke, just off the Isle of Wight. Although damaged the ship was able to limp back to Southampton. At the inquiry, the Royal Navy blamed the Olympic for the incident, alleging that her large displacement generated a suction that pulled HMS Hawke into her side.

On 10th April 1912, Violet boarded RMS Titanic to serve as stewardess on her maiden voyage to New York. When the Titanic hit an iceberg four days later, Violet was ordered into lifeboat no 16, and, as the boat was being lowered, one of the Titanic's officers gave her a baby to look after. The next morning, Violet and the rest of the survivors were rescued by the RMS Carpathia.

On the morning of 21st November 1916, Violet was on board HMHS Britannic when the ship apparently struck a sea mine and, with all the portholes open for ventilation, she quickly sank, off the Greek island of Kea, with the loss of 30 lives. Violet jumped out of a lifeboat to avoid being sucked into the ship's propellers. Sucked under the water anyway, she struck her head on the ship's keel before surfacing and being rescued by a lifeboat. She later said that the cushioning afforded to her by her thick auburn hair helped save her life.

After the war, Violet continued to work on cruise ships, retiring in 1950. She died in 1971 at the age of 83.

With millions of men away fighting and, with the inevitable casualties, there was a severe shortage of labour during the war. By 1914, over 5 million British women were working. Hundreds of thousands worked in munitions factories, offices and aircraft hangars. For the duration of the war, women took on many of the traditional male work roles. However, in accordance with the agreement negotiated with the trade unions, women undertaking those jobs lost them at the end of the war.

Many women were also heavily involved in voluntary work, for example, knitting socks for the soldiers on the front, encouraging the sale of war bonds, working at Red Cross depots across the country organising the supply of hospital clothing and essential medical supplies and parcels for prisoners of war.

The Women's Land Army, or WLA, was a British organisation created during the war to place women volunteers on farms who needed labour to replace agricultural workers away at war. The WLA women were commonly known as Land Girls. Many traditional farmers were initially against the idea but were encouraged to accept women's work on the farms. Towards the end of 1917 there were over 250,000 women working as farm labourers.

Munitions work was highly paid but had an inherent risk; exposure to the explosive, TNT. It was common practice for women to pack TNT into shell casings by hand. TNT caused headaches and nausea as well as staining the skin and hair yellow, earning women the nickname, *Canary Girls*. In the worst cases, TNT poisoning caused organ failure and death. Around 400 women died from overexposure to TNT. Charlotte Meade, known as Lottie, seen left, was a munitions worker. She died on 11 October 1916 in Kensington Infirmary. Her death certificate states the cause of death as: *coma due to disease of the liver, heart and kidneys consequent upon poisoning by tri nitro toluene.*

MS I have always had a great love of book arts and I'm particularly passionate about altered books. I adore books, new and old, and I love to read. As an art form, altered books have huge potential, they can be made by all ages, using any media or techniques. There are no rules for altered books and they offer exceptional creative freedom. Many see altered books as a disrespectful and irreverent activity having been taught in childhood never to mark a book. I, however, see a superb opportunity to breathe new life into a care worn object, to transform an unloved book, destined for the scrap heap, into a work of art. *The Munitionette* is created with a German novel.

The Munitionette by Marian Savill

Nursing was almost the only area of female contribution that involved being at the front, experiencing the war. In Britain, the Queen Alexandra's Imperial Military Nursing Service (QUAIMS), First Aid Nursing Yeomanry (FANY) and Voluntary Aid Detachment (VAD) provided nurses. The VADs were not allowed in the front line until 1915.

Over 2,800 women served with the Royal Canadian Army Medical Corps. It was during this conflict that the role of Canadian women in the military went beyond nursing. Women were trained in the use of small arms; 43 died during the war. The Americans had more than 12,000 women enlisted in the Navy and Marine Corps during the war, with about 400 of them being killed. The only country to deploy female combat troops in substantial numbers was Russia in 1917. Its *Women's Battalions* fought well, but failed to provide the propaganda value expected and were disbanded before the end of the year.

Captain Flora Sandes, from Nether Poppleton in Yorkshire, was the only British woman to officially serve as a front-line soldier. She joined the St John Ambulance as a volunteer and, in 1914, she travelled to Serbia, where, in the confusion of war, she was formally enrolled in the Serbian army.

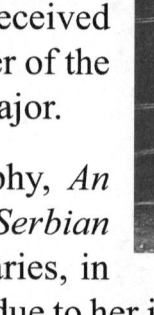

In 1916, during the Serbian advance on Bitola, Sandes was seriously wounded by a grenade. She subsequently received the highest decoration of the Serbian Military, the Order of the Karađorđe's Star and was promoted to the Sergeant Major.

Sandes published her autobiography, *An English Woman-Sergeant in the Serbian Army*, based on her letters and diaries, in 1916. Unable to continue fighting due to her injury, she spent the remainder of the war running a hospital. At the end of the war she was commissioned as a Captain, the first woman to be commissioned, and was finally demobilised in October 1922. In 1927, she published a second autobiography. She lectured extensively on her wartime experiences around the world, wearing her military uniform.

She spent the last years of her life in Suffolk, where she died in November 1956, aged 80.

The massive contribution of women during the war was a factor in them gaining the right to vote. The roots of woman's suffrage are as long as the injustice of inequality. In Britain, the National Union of Women's Suffrage Societies was formed in 1897. In 1903, the more militant Women's Social and Political Union was founded, splitting from the NUWSS, and led by mother and daughter, Emmeline and Sylvia Pankhurst. Over 1,000 suffragettes went to prison for militant acts, such as criminal damage to property, chaining themselves to railings and attacking works of art, to draw attention to the cause. Despite his support for women's suffrage, the Chancellor of Exchequer, David Lloyd George's house was bombed by the WSPU. In prison, suffragettes were not classed as political prisoners but as common criminals. Many imprisoned suffragettes went on hunger strike as a protest against this treatment and were violently force fed. On 4th June 1913, Emily Davison stepped in front of King George V's horse, Anmer, at the Epsom Derby. Four days later, she died from her injuries and the suffrage movement had their first martyr.

At the outbreak of the war, the WSPU called for the cessation of militant activities and for full support for the British government in war. During the war, lobbying took place behind the scenes and there was a growing feeling within parliament that women deserved greater political rights.

In 1918, the Representation of the People Act 1918 was passed, giving women over the age of 30, who met minimum property qualifications, the right to vote. The Representation of the People Act 1928 extended the voting franchise to all women over the age of 21.

 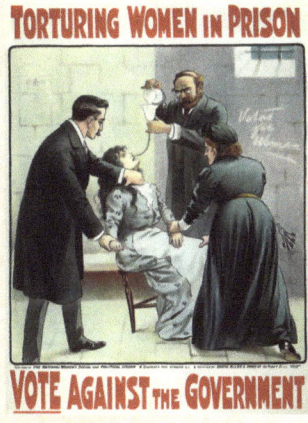  

The Worst Friend and Enemy by Marian Savill

Detail from The Worst Friend and Enemy by Marian Savill

MS As a woman in the modern day world of mobile phones, email and Skype, to name a few, it is very difficult to imagine the constant anguish and worry women suffered during the war. The strain of not knowing the whereabouts of husbands, brothers, sons and friends, not knowing if they were dead or alive or mortally wounded, must have been immense. Carrying on with daily life under those stressful circumstances must have tested their strength continually. With *The Worst Friend and Enemy* I wanted to explore the expression of this female turmoil in textural paint as well as collage.

> From One Who Stays
>
> How empty seems the town now you are gone!
> A wilderness of sad streets, where gaunt walls
> Hide nothing to desire; sunshine falls
> Eery, distorted, as it long had shone
> On white, dead faces tombed in halls of stone.
> The whir of motors, stricken through with calls
> Of playing boys, floats up at intervals;
> But all these noises blur to one long moan.
> What quest is worth pursuing? And how strange
> That other men still go accustomed ways!
> I hate their interest in the things they do.
> A spectre-horde repeating without change
> An old routine. Alone I know the days
> Are still-born, and the world stopped, lacking you.
>
> Amy Lowell

Je suis une brave poule de guerre by Marian Savill

MS This collage is my take on one of the many war time posters, seen opposite, which fascinated me, both in graphic design and subject matter. The text translates as *I am a brave chicken of war, I eat little and produce much*. There were many propaganda posters on the topic of food, designed to encourage thrifty ways.

The war was drawing to a close before food rationing was introduced in the UK. Every nation involved in the war suffered hunger and food shortages. Many countries relied heavily on wheat imports and German submarine warfare on ships carrying essential supplies had a devastating effect; food prices rose and long queues to buy food were commonplace. At the beginning of 1918, food rationing was introduced in London and the Home Counties with most of the rest of the country brought in by April. Meat, bacon, butter/margarine and sugar were rationed, and the availability of other foods was also controlled by the Government. Food queuing and soaring prices eased with rationing in place and the health of many people improved.

Siegfried Sassoon, CBE, MC was an English poet, writer and soldier who was decorated for bravery on the Western Front. His poetry was angry and compassionate, depicting the horrors of the trenches, and contemptuous of those who were, in his view, responsible for a *jingoism-fuelled war*. Commissioned into the Royal Welsh Fusiliers as a second lieutenant, in November 1915, he was sent to France.

He showed exceptional bravery in France, including single-handedly capturing a German trench in daylight, under covering fire from a couple of rifles. His men nicknamed him *Mad Jack* for his near-suicidal exploits. On 27th July 1916, he was awarded the Military Cross.

In 1917, Sassoon made a stand against the war. At the end of a spell of convalescence, he declined to return to duty and sent a letter to his commanding officer which included:

I am making this statement as an act of wilful defiance of military authority, because I believe that the war is being deliberately prolonged by those who have the power to end it.

Rather than being arrested, Sassoon was sent to Craiglockhart War Hospital where he was officially treated for *shell shock*. While there he met fellow poet, Wilfred Owen, whose work he was later instrumental in bringing to a wider audience. Back on active service, in 1918, Sassoon was wounded again and spent the remainder of the war in Britain.

Sassoon died one week before his 81st birthday, in 1967, and is among sixteen Great War poets commemorated in Westminster Abbey's Poet's Corner.

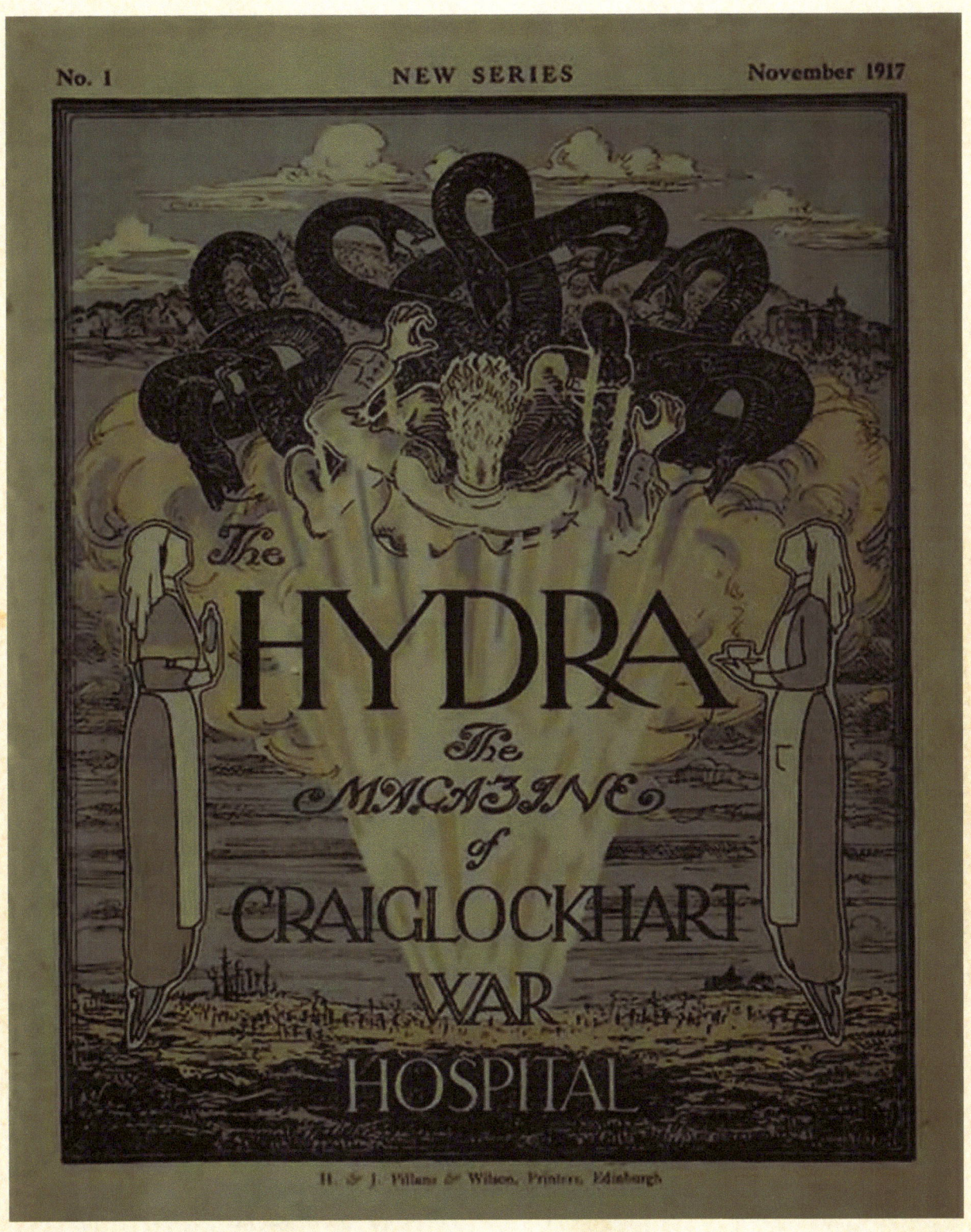

The Hydra Magazine was produced by the patients of the Craiglockhart, a war hospital, in Edinburgh, for officers suffering from psychological trauma. Wilfred Owen edited the magazine for a time and Siegfried Sassoon contributed his poem, Dreamers, for inclusion.

Wilfred Owen, MC, was one of the leading poets of the war. His poetry was shocking, and realistic, graphically describing the horrors of the trenches and gas warfare. They stood in stark contrast to the public perception of war at the time. Among his best known works, nearly all published posthumously, are *Dulce et Decorum Est*, *Insensibility*, *Anthem for Doomed Youth*, *Futility* and *Strange Meeting*.

Particularly inspired by John Keats, Owen discovered his poetic vocation while on holiday in Cheshire. In 1913, he was working as a private tutor teaching English and French in Bordeaux, France. In 1915, Owen enlisted in the Artists Rifles Officer Training Corps. Commissioned as a second lieutenant in the Manchester Regiment in June 1916, he was sent to France. After several traumatic experiences, including spending several days lying in the open after being blown sky high by a trench mortar, he was diagnosed as suffering from shell shock and sent to Craiglockhart War Hospital in Edinburgh for treatment. It was there he met fellow poet, Siegfried Sassoon, who became friend and mentor to him and heavily influenced his poetry. Owen returned to France in 1918 and was killed in action one week before the end of the war, his parents received the news of his death on Armistice Day as the bells of the local church were ringing in celebration. He was awarded the Military Cross for conspicuous gallantry and devotion to duty during an attack near Joncourt.

Owen is also one of the Great War poets commemorated in Westminster Abbey's Poet's Corner. The inscription on the stone is taken from Owen's *Preface* and reads:

> *My subject is War, and the pity of War. The Poetry is in the pity*

English poet, Rupert Brooke is best known for his idealistic war sonnets. Before the war, Brooke made friends amongst the Bloomsbury group of writers, where he was admired for his talent as well as his good looks. Virginia Woolf boasted to Vita Sackville-West of once skinny-dipping with Brooke when they were at Cambridge together.

Commissioned into the Royal Naval Volunteer Reserve, Brooke sailed with the British Mediterranean Expeditionary Force on 28th February 1915 destined for the Gallipoli campaign, but he developed sepsis from an infected mosquito bite and died on a hospital ship moored off the island of Skyros on 23rd April. The first of the war poets to die, Brooke never experienced the trenches and his poems reflect the idealised, romantic, patriotism prevalent at the beginning of the war.

The Soldier

If I should die, think only this of me:
That there's some corner of a foreign field
That is for ever England. There shall be
In that rich earth a richer dust concealed;
A dust whom England bore, shaped, made aware,
Gave once her flowers to love, her ways to roam;
A body of England's, breathing English air,
Washed by the rivers, blest by suns of home.
And think, this heart, all evil shed away,
A pulse in the eternal mind, no less
Gives somewhere back the thoughts by England given;
Her sights and sounds; dreams happy as her day;
And laughter, learnt of friends; and gentleness,
In hearts at peace, under an English heaven.

Rupert Brooke

Ivor Gurney was an English composer and poet. Musically talented from an early age he began composing at the age of 14 and won a scholarship to the Royal College of Music. His studies were interrupted by the war and, in 1915, he enlisted in the Gloucestershire Regiment.

At the front, he began writing poetry. He had started work on what would become his first book *Severn and Somme*, when he was wounded in the shoulder in April 1917. Returning to battle, he continued working on his book and composing music including the songs, *In Flanders* and *By A Bierside*. In September 1917, Gurney was gassed and sent to the Edinburgh War Hospital and then posted to a Northumberland village, where he continued to write.

In 1918, he suffered a serious breakdown, and was given the unusual diagnosis of *nervous breakdown from deferred shell shock*. He continued to compose and write but his mental health deteriorated and, in 1922, his family had him declared insane. He spent the last 15 years of his life in mental hospitals where he died of tuberculosis in 1937, aged 47.

Ernest Hemingway, American author and journalist, served as an ambulance driver in Italy during 1918. On his first day in Milan, he was ordered to a munitions factory which had exploded. He was confronted by the shredded remains of female workers. He described the scene in the non-fiction book, *Death in the Afternoon: I remember that after we searched quite thoroughly for the complete dead, we collected fragments*.

Soon after, he was seriously wounded by mortar fire. His war time experiences were the basis for his 1929 novel, *A Farewell to Arms*, his first bestseller. Hemingway was a war correspondent in the Second World War. He had 20+ books published and won the Pulitzer Prize for Fiction in 1953 and the Nobel Prize for Literature in 1954.

Ernst Toller was a German Jewish left wing playwright and poet, best known for his Expressionist plays.

At the outbreak of war, Toller volunteered for military duty and served just over a year before suffering a complete physical and mental breakdown. His first drama, *Transformation,* published in 1919, was prompted by his wartime experiences.

He served for six days as President of the short-lived Bavarian Soviet Republic and was imprisoned for five years for his actions. Whilst incarcerated, he wrote several plays and poetry which earned him international renown. In 1933, Toller was exiled from Germany after the Nazis came to power and settled in New York, joining other exiles there. Struggling financially and depressed at the news that his siblings had been sent to concentration camps in Germany, he committed suicide in May 1939.

Thomas Edward Lawrence, CB, DSO, was a British Army officer renowned for his liaison role during the Sinai and Palestine Campaign and the Arab Revolt against Ottoman Turkish rule of 1916–18. His activities and his talent for describing them vividly in writing, earned him international fame as *Lawrence of Arabia*, a title which was used for the 1962 film based on his activities during the war.

Before the war, Lawrence studied history and became a practising archaeologist in the Middle East travelling extensively in the area. In 1914, he enlisted and was sent to the intelligence staff in Cairo. He fought alongside Arab irregular troops in extended guerrilla operations against the armed forces of the Ottoman Empire and was promoted to Major. Lawrence's autobiographical account of his war experiences, *Seven Pillars of Wisdom*, was published in 1922. He is one of the very few Englishmen who have ever refused both a knighthood and the Victoria Cross. A keen motorcyclist, Lawrence was fatally injured in a motorcycle accident near his Dorset home in 1935.

MS Richard and I have very different working practices. I'm something of a hunter/gatherer artist, in that the very nature of assemblage and collage means I browse and sort through potential objects and materials creating small vignettes in the studio which I can add to, take from, move around and use to prompt ideas. I also use sketchbooks and vision boards to develop ideas and think out loud visually before, during and, sometimes after, the creation of a piece. Examples from some of my First World War explorations can be seen above. Much of my exploratory work is not intended as blueprints for pieces but, rather, as a way to develop emotive responses to the subject matter before creating new work.

Otto Dix was a German painter and printmaker, noted for his unforgiving and brutally realistic depictions of the war. Exposed to art from an early age, Dix served an apprenticeship with a painter and studied at the Academy of Applied Arts in Dresden before the war.

Dix volunteered for the German Army at the outbreak of war in a field artillery regiment. In 1915, he was assigned to a machine-gun unit and took part in the Battle of the Somme. He served on the French and Russian fronts until 1918 and was awarded an Iron Cross. Dix was profoundly affected by the experience of the war, which reflected in his art. With the rise of Nazism in the 1930s, Dix was labelled as a degenerate artist and sacked from the Dresden Academy. In 1937, his paintings, *The Trench* and *War Cripples,* were confiscated and exhibited in the state sponsored, *Degenerate Art Exhibition* in Munich. They were later burned. In 1939, he was arrested on a charge of being involved in a plot against Hitler, but was later released. Dix returned to Dresden eventually and remained there until 1966. He died in 1969 after a second stroke.

Christopher Nevinson, born in 1889, became one of the most famous artists of the war. He attended the Slade School of Art in London where he was advised by his Professor of Drawing, Henry Tonks, that he should abandon all thought of a career as an artist.

Nevinson joined the Friends' Ambulance Unit at the outbreak of war and tended wounded French soldiers, work that he found deeply disturbing. He also worked briefly as an ambulance driver as well as for the Red Cross and Royal Army Medical Corps. These experiences became the subject matter for a series of powerful paintings which used Futurist techniques to great effect. He was eventually appointed as a war artist although his later paintings lacked the impact of his earlier war work. Post war, Nevinson abandoned Futurism and his subsequent more conventional work is generally regarded as lacklustre. Interestingly, Nevinson is credited with holding the first cocktail party in Britain in 1924. He died in 1946 from heart disease.

Bruce Bairnsfather, humorist and cartoonist, became famous during the war for being the creator of *Old Bill*, a much loved cartoon character featured in *Fragments from France*, published weekly in *The Bystander*

Born into a military family in Murree, now in Pakistan, Bairnsfather enlisted in 1914, joining the Royal Warwickshire Regiment, and served with a machine gun unit in France until 1915 when he was hospitalised with shell shock and hearing damage sustained during the Second Battle of Ypres. Before the war, he studied at the John Hassall School of Art. He was introduced to Thomas Lipton, which led to commissions to draw advertising sketches for Lipton Tea, Player's Cigarettes, Keen's Mustard, and Beecham's Pills.

His character *Old Bill*, was a curmudgeonly soldier with a trademark walrus moustache and balaclava. Old Bill, and Bairnsfather, continued to be popular between the World Wars. In the Second World War, he became official cartoonist to the American forces in Europe, contributing to Stars and Stripes and Yank, drawing cartoons at American bases and nose art on aircraft.

He died in 1959 at the age of 72.

"Well, if yer knows of a better 'ole, go to it!"

Paul Nash was a British surrealist painter and war artist. Born in London in 1889, he was destined for a career in the navy, following in the footsteps of his maternal grandfather, but after failing his exams he decided to pursue art as a career.

Influenced by the poetry of William Blake and the work of Dante Gabriel Rossetti and Samuel Palmer, Nash was starting to enjoy some success with his drawings and watercolours of brooding landscapes before the war.

Nash reluctantly enlisted in the Artists Rifles at the start of the war and was sent to France in February 1917 as a second lieutenant in the Hampshire Regiment. Just before the Ypres offensive began, he fell into a trench, broke a rib and was invalided home. While recovering, Nash produced a series of war drawings from his front line sketches. Consequently, he was recruited as an official war artist and returned to the Western Front where his drawings led to his first oil paintings. Nash's paintings *The Menin Road, We Are Making a New World, The Ypres Salient at Night* and *Wire* are among the most iconic and lasting images of the war. After the war, Nash was a pioneer of modernism in Britain, and continued painting as well as illustrating books and photography In the Second World War he was again an official war artist. He died from heart failure in 1946.

The Artist Rifles

The Battle of Jutland, *Skagerrakschlacht* to the Germans, was a naval battle fought by the Royal Navy's Grand Fleet against the Imperial German Navy's High Seas Fleet. Fought on 31st May and 1st June 1916 in the North Sea, near Jutland, Denmark, it was the largest naval engagement of the war. The Grand Fleet was commanded by British Admiral, Sir John Jellicoe, and the High Seas Fleet by German Vice-Admiral, Reinhard Scheer. The High Seas Fleet intended to lure out, trap and destroy a portion of the Grand Fleet. This formed part of a German strategy to break the British blockade of Germany and to allow mercantile shipping to operate. Meanwhile, the Royal Navy were in pursuit of engaging and destroying the High Seas Fleet, keeping it away from Britain's own shipping lanes.

Admiral Von Scheer

The German plan was to lure Vice-Admiral Sir David Beatty's battlecruiser squadrons into the path of the main German fleet. Submarines were stationed in advance across the likely routes of the British ships. The British intercepted signals and learned of the plan. On 30th May, Jellicoe sailed with the Grand Fleet to rendezvous with Beatty, passing over the German submarine lines while they were unprepared which created problems for the submarines which had reached the limit of their endurance at sea.

On 31st May, Beatty encountered the German force and a running battle ensued. By the time Beatty sighted the larger German fleet, he had lost two of his six battlecruisers and four battleships. He withdrew, heading to the main British fleet with the German ships in pursuit. As night fell, intense fighting ensued between the two fleets, totalling 250 ships. Fourteen British ships and eleven German ships were sunk, with nearly 9000 men killed and another 1000 wounded. Overnight, Jellicoe manoeuvred to cut the Germans off in the hope of continuing the battle, but under the cover of darkness the German fleet broke through the British rearguard and returned to port.

Admiral
Sir John Jellicoe

Both sides claimed victory of the battle. The British lost more ships and sailors than the German fleet and Beatty and Jellicoe were heavily criticised but the British Navy were ready for action again the next day whereas Germany never really challenged Britain at sea during the war again .

RMS Lusitania, launched by the Cunard Line in 1907, was a British ocean liner, holder of the Blue Riband and, briefly, the world's biggest ship. When she left New York for Liverpool on what would be her final voyage on 1st May 1915, submarine warfare was intensifying in the Atlantic. The German Embassy in America had placed a newspaper advertisement warning people not to sail on the Lusitania. On the afternoon of 7th May, the Lusitania was torpedoed by a German U-Boat, 11 miles off the south coast of Ireland. A second internal explosion sent her to the bottom of the ocean in just 18 minutes with the loss of 1,198 passengers. In firing on a non-military ship without warning, the Germans had breached the international laws known as the Cruiser Rules. Although the Germans had cause to treat the Lusitania as a naval vessel, including the fact that she was carrying munitions, and the British had also been breaching the Cruiser Rules, the sinking caused a storm of protest in the United States and influenced the decision by the US to declare war in 1917.

The Sinking of the Lusitania by Richard Savage and Marian Savill

The Hope of Just One More by Richard Savage

A Wolf on the Prowl by Richard Savage

The first German submarine was designed in 1850 and had a three man crew. It sank to the bottom of Kiel harbour during its first test dive. In 1903, Germaniawerft dockyard in Kiel completed Germany's first fully functional submarine. At the start of the war, Germany had 29 U-boats and in the first ten weeks, five British cruisers were lost to them. On 5th September 1914, HMS Pathfinder was sunk by U-21, the first ship to have been sunk by a submarine using a self-propelled torpedo. U-9 sank the British warships HMS Aboukir, HMS Cressy and HMS Hogue in a single hour. After the Armistice, all surviving German submarines were surrendered. In total, 360 submarines were built and 178 were lost. Over the course of the war more than 11 million tons of shipping was lost to German U-Boat attacks.

THE WATCHERS OF THE SEAS.
THE NAVY NEEDS BOYS AND MEN FROM 15 TO 40 YEARS OF AGE.
APPLY: 7, WHITEHALL PLACE, S.W.

British B Class submarines were built by Vickers in Barrow-in-Furness. Their surface speed was 12 knots, submerged speed was 6 knots, with a range of 1,000 nautical miles. The submarines had a crew of fifteen and were armed with four 18 inch torpedos.

The K class Royal Navy submarines, propelled by steam, were designed in 1913. They earned the nickname, *Kalamity class*, for being involved in numerous accidents. Of the 18 that were built none were lost in enemy action but six sank in accidents. Only one ever engaged an enemy vessel, hitting a U-boat amidships, though the torpedo failed to explode. In one incident, HMS Fearless, a cruiser, collided with K17, which sank in about 8 minutes. The submarines behind made evasive manoeuvres; K4 was struck by K6, which almost cut her in half, and was then struck by K7 before she finally sank with all her crew. At the same time, K22 and K14 collided although both craft survived. In just 75 minutes, two submarines had been sunk, three badly damaged and 105 crew killed.

I Will Return by Marian Savill

MS For me, one of the fascinations of working alongside another artist is seeing how differently we deal with materials, how each of us has such unique working techniques and how, from the same starting point, we can produce two pieces of such wonderfully disparate work. This was the case when we began *Above Us the Waves* and *I Will Return*. My piece was borne of a serendipitous mistake when I added far too much white acrylic paint to the canvas. In the process of cleaning off the excess paint the effect I created was very pleasing so I continued removing paint, in some areas right back down to the canvas. The collage piece adds a human element to the swirling, organic background.

Above Us the Waves by Richard Savage

RS I found the process of working together, yet separately, strangely liberating; as my solo working practice is very different. When setting out a traditional painting there is, for me, preliminary work, source material and setting out of the subject matter. *Above Us the Waves* broke with my usual conventions; I elected to use a palette knife to apply paint in deep textural layers, waves of colour, mixed directly on the canvas with subsequent additional layers of over painting across the canvas. I love the effect of movement, a captured moment, the feeling of a person cast into water; confusion and panic. In a strange way the surface patination evokes a feeling of claustrophobia.

The Hague Conventions of 1899 and 1907 set out conditions and rules that governed prisoners of war, from the conditions they lived in to the food they ate. At the time the rules were written nobody had anticipated the possible scale of future wars. Prisoners of war in Europe numbered approximately seven million, around a third of which were held by Germany. With such numbers it was impossible to fully respect the conventions in their smallest details.

Germany found themselves inundated with prisoners from the start of the war and consequently the conditions were haphazard and poorly organised. In 1915, the German authorities organised a system of nearly three hundred camps to hold their captives.

In 1916, newly captured British and French prisoners were used as forced labour on the Eastern Front in response to the French sending German prisoners of war to camps in North Africa and the British using German prisoners as forced labour in France. This caused escalated reprisals on the Eastern Front with horrific incidents of brutality and many prisoners dying of cold and starvation on both sides. These reprisals marked a significant rise in prisoner of war mistreatment. In 1921, under the terms of the Treaty of Versailles, a series of trials for alleged German war criminals were held. Twelve men were accused of mistreating prisoners. Four were found guilty and sentenced to terms in prison.

Top, German prisoners behind barbed wire. Below, British and Portuguese prisoners of war

Holzminden prisoner of war camp, in Lower Saxony, was opened in September 1917. The camp held between 500 and 600 officers and 100 to 160 other ranks. It was the location of the largest escape attempt of prisoners during the war. The Daily Sketch described it as *the worst camp in Germany* and escape attempts were commonplace, some as simple as cutting the perimeter fence or walking through the gates disguised as a guard, civilian worker, or, on at least one occasion, a woman. Many of these escapes were successful, but virtually all the escapees were recaptured within a matter of days. The most celebrated escape was through a tunnel in July 1918. The tunnel had taken nine months to dig and 86 officers were on the escape list. The 30th man unfortunately became stuck in the tunnel but ten of the twenty nine escapees, including Colonel Charles Rathborne, the Senior British Officer in the camp, succeeded in making their way back to Britain. The camp closed in December 1918 and the prisoners were repatriated. The two main barrack blocks survive and are still in military use by the German Army.

Some of the notable prisoners at the camp were:
Edward Donald Bellew, VC, Commander Edward Bingham, VC, Algernon Frederick Bird, 61st victim of the Red Baron, Michael Claude Hamilton Bowes-Lyon, son of the 14th Earl of Strathmore and Kinghorne and brother of the future Queen Elizabeth The Queen Mother, Christopher Guy Gilbert, 31st victim of the Red Baron, Brian Horrocks, World War II British army general, William Leefe Robinson, VC, the first British pilot to shoot down a German airship over Britain and James Whale, later to be Hollywood film director.

PALS!

The contribution of animals to the war was more varied and numerous than generally imagined. The current popularity of *War Horse* has secured the place of horses in the history of the war but many other animals were involved in the conflict.

A quote connected with the Maginot Line is: *generals always fight the last war, especially if they have won it*, and the number of horses used at the start of the war were on the scale of the Napoleonic War.

Britain and Germany each had cavalry forces of about 100,000 men. All senior military personnel at this time believed in the supremacy of the cavalry attack and cavalry regiments would have been seen as the senior regiments in the British Army, along with the Guards regiments, and many senior army positions were held by cavalry officers. Horses were involved in the war's first major action, the Battle of Mons in August 1914. Due to the nature of trench warfare though cavalry charges were no longer a viable military tactic. In March 1918, however, the British launched a cavalry charge at the Germans. Out of the 150 horses used in the charge only 4 survived. The rest were cut down by German machine gun fire.

The Animals in War Memorial by sculptor David Backhouse in Hyde Park, London

Horses were still invaluable at the front though; for reconnaissance and messengers as well as pulling artillery, ambulances and supply wagons. Mechanised vehicles, were relatively new inventions and prone to constant breakdowns. Horses, along with mules, were much more reliable. Britain lost over half a million horses during the war.

The Road to Salvation by Richard Savage

Dogs played a vital role in the war. It is estimated that by 1918, Germany had employed 30,000 dogs, Britain, France and Belgian over 20,000 and Italy 3000. America, at first, did not use dogs except for a few hundred from the Allies for specific missions, although the USA produced the most decorated and highly ranked service dog in military history, Sergeant Stubby.

Sergeant Stubby fought in 17 battles. He was in the trenches in France for 18 months, survived being gassed and went on to warn his unit of incoming gas attacks and artillery shelling. He also helped to locate wounded soldiers after bombardments and, on one notable occasion, helped capture a German spy. After the war, Stubby became the Georgetown Hoyas' football team mascot. Sergeant Stubby has a brick in the Walk of Honor at the United States World War One monument in Kansas City.

Lots of dog breeds were used during the war, the most popular being medium sized, intelligent and trainable breeds. Doberman Pinschers and German Shepherds, were most popularly used although smaller terrier breeds were employed as ratters and trained to hunt and kill rats in the trenches. Dogs also acted as sentry, guard and scout dogs. Scout dogs worked with soldiers on foot, patrolling the terrain ahead of them. They could detect enemy scents up to 1000 yards away and indicate without barking.

Casualty or *mercy dogs* were trained to find wounded and dying men on the battlefields and were equipped with medical supplies. Soldiers who could help themselves to the supplies would tend to their own wounds, or dogs would stay with the more gravely injured for comfort until stretcher bearers reached them.

Dogs proved to be reliable messengers. Trained dogs moved much faster than men, presented a harder target for snipers and could travel over any terrain. One dog travelled 2 1/2 miles on the Western Front, with an important message to a brigade's headquarters, over very difficult terrain, in less than sixty minutes.

Dogs also played a vital humanitarian role on the Western Front. For men trapped in the horrors of trench warfare, a dog was a psychological comfort that took away, if only for a short time, the horrors they lived through. For many soldiers a dog in the trenches must have reminded them of home comforts.

Many more unusual animals were adopted as lucky mascots during the war; cats, goats, a fox, a monkey, an owl and a hedgehog all numbered among the menagerie.

A German solider transporting pigeons

Communication systems at this time were still crude and often unreliable and pigeons proved to be an extremely good way of sending messages. Over 100,000 pigeons were used in the war with a success rate of 95% getting through to their destination with their message.

At the First Battle of the Marne in 1914, French troops stopped the German advance on Paris. In the confusion of battle, pigeons proved to be the best way of sending messages to the French headquarters. The French had 72 pigeon lofts and carried them forward with them as they advanced. Many of the pigeons were carrying messages at the time so would have had no idea where their loft had been moved to but, amazingly, all the pigeons returned to their lofts. Such was the importance of pigeons to the war effort that killing, wounding or molesting homing pigeons was a breach of the Defence of the Realm Regulation 21a and was punishable by six months imprisonment or a fine of £100.

A motorised pigeon loft

Seen bove, the highly unusual sight of a field being ploughed by an elephant commandeered by the German army from a Belgian zoo in 1915.

107

The term *shell shock* became synonymous with this period. The same term was used for two quite different conditions though. The first, neurasthenia, a term originally used in the 1830s as a mechanical weakness of the physical fibres of the nerves. In 1869, George Miller Beard altered the medical definition of neurasthenia to denote symptoms of fatigue, anxiety, headache, neuralgia and a depressed mood. Cambridge psychologist and Army medical officer, Charles Myers, was the first person to use the phrase shell shock in The Lancet in relation to psychological trauma. The second use of the term is the result of psychological trauma following a physical injury to the nerves such as being hit by shock waves from a heavy bombardment or being buried alive. Symptoms of this physical shell shock could include tinnitus, amnesia, uncontrollable diarrhoea, headache, facial tics and dizziness.

Accounts from the British Medical Journal from the time, tell of conflicts of medical opinion between the two conditions and misdiagnoses of both. The topic was further complicated by the fact that a person suffering from the one condition did not preclude them from suffering from the other condition at the same time.

Initially, shell shock casualties were quickly evacuated from the front line, partly because of their unpredictability. By the Battle of Passchendaele in 1917, methods had been developed to try and reduce shell shock. If a soldier began to show symptoms of neurasthenia, the recommended course of action was for the Medical Officer to give him a few days of rest away from the front line. If symptoms persisted men were sent to psychiatric centres for assessment.

During the war, there were tens of thousands of cases of both kinds of shell shock, four-fifths of men who had entered hospital suffering shell shock were never able to return to military duty. Some British military hospitals were set up specifically to treat shell shock. Treatments varied including simple rest, massage, dietary regimes and electric shock treatment. As the medical superintendent at one military hospital in York put it, *although the medical officer must show sympathy, the patient must be induced to face his illness in a manly way*. Sympathy was rarely forthcoming in the army or when the shell shocked men returned home.

Post war, thousands of veterans still received treatment for psychological trauma. The term shell shock was banned as a diagnosis in the British Army. After 1918, the term neurasthenia was referred to as *Combat Stress Reaction*, or *CSR*, within the military to describe the acute trauma of war, also known as *combat fatigue*, which, in turn, overlaps with *post-traumatic stress disorder*.

Quiet Desperation is the English Way by Richard Savage and Marian Savill

Some men suffering from shell shock were put on trial, and even executed, for desertion and cowardice.

Although it was recognised that men could crack under the strain of war, long term symptoms were seen as lack of character and shell shock was not an admissible defence. Many thousands of men were court-martialled during the war and just over 3,000 were sentenced to death, however in 90% of cases, the sentence was commuted to hard labour or penal servitude.

In November 2006, the British government granted all the executed soldiers posthumous conditional pardons.

The Darkness of Despair by Richard Savage and Marian Savill

RS This kinetic painting uses multiple layers of thinly applied ribbons of paint. For me, the joy of working with another artist on these paintings is two individuals, two minds, neither of us talking as we work, and yet the art seems to materialise from somewhere independent but still connected to both of us. We could both do this work alone, but I can't imagine ever wanting to do so.

MS The iconic, enduring image of the poppy was one I felt compelled to explore in collage. Working with magazine and old book pages to create a realistic poppy was an interesting process. A lot of my collage work is abstract and working in a representational way can be challenging for me but it's always a pleasurable experience. Sorting through papers, selecting the required colours and tonal values, is an important yet time consuming part of the process but it is vital for attuning the eye to the various shades and hues of colour I want to use in a piece. As in most forms of artwork, I create the background first and work forward giving it's three dimensional appearance.

In Flanders Fields

In Flanders fields the poppies blow
Between the crosses, row on row,
That mark our place; and in the sky
The larks, still bravely singing, fly
Scarce heard amid the guns below.

We are the Dead. Short days ago
We lived, felt dawn, saw sunset glow,
Loved and were loved, and now we lie
In Flanders fields.

Take up our quarrel with the foe:
To you from failing hands we throw
The torch; be yours to hold it high.
If ye break faith with us who die
We shall not sleep, though poppies grow
In Flanders fields.

In Flanders Fields by Marian Savill

John McCrae

The Cenotaph

Not yet will those measureless fields be green again
Where only yesterday the wild sweet blood of wonderful youth was shed;
There is a grave whose earth must hold too long, too deep a stain,
Though for ever over it we may speak as proudly as we may tread.
But here, where the watchers by lonely hearths from the thrust of an inward sword have more slowly bled,
We shall build the Cenotaph: Victory, winged, with Peace, winged too, at the column's head.
And over the stairway, at the foot—oh! here, leave desolate, passionate hands to spread
Violets, roses, and laurel, with the small sweet tinkling country things
Speaking so wistfully of other Springs
From the little gardens of little places where son or sweetheart was born and bred.
In splendid sleep, with a thousand brothers
To lovers—to mothers
Here, too, lies he:
Under the purple, the green, the red,
It is all young life: it must break some women's hearts to see
Such a brave, gay coverlet to such a bed!
Only, when all is done and said,
God is not mocked and neither are the dead.
For this will stand in our Market-place—
Who'll sell, who'll buy
(Will you or I
Lie each to each with the better grace)?
While looking into every busy whore's and huckster's face
As they drive their bargains, is the Face
Of God: and some young, piteous, murdered face.

Charlotte Mew

End of the Shift by Richard Savage

By the end of the war, almost one million British soldiers, sailors and airmen had been killed. In addition, nearly two million more had been permanently disabled, with over 40,000 losing limbs and all needed ongoing medical treatment. Provision to reintegrate disabled service personnel back into work or give financial support was also needed. Many new charities were formed to help ex-servicemen, The Royal British Legion and The Disabled Society being two examples.

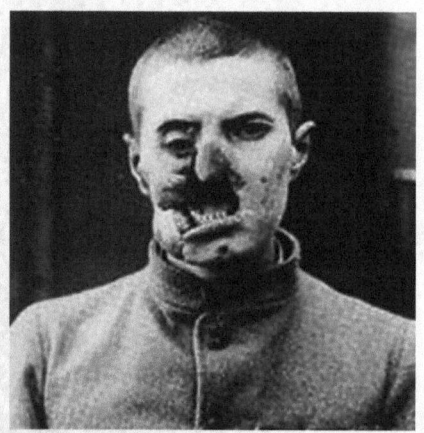

Plastic surgeon, Sir Harold Gillies, pioneered facial repair surgery at the Queen's Hospital, Sidcup, Kent. Many soldiers had horrifically damaged faces from gunshot and shrapnel injuries. Gillies performed flap surgery to great functional and aesthetic effect. He also worked with artist, Francis Derwent-Wood, to create masks for burned patients whose faces could not be fully restored by surgery.

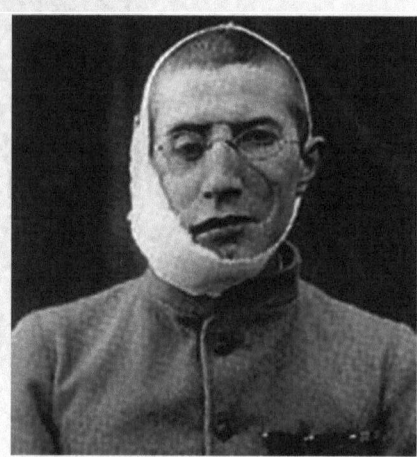
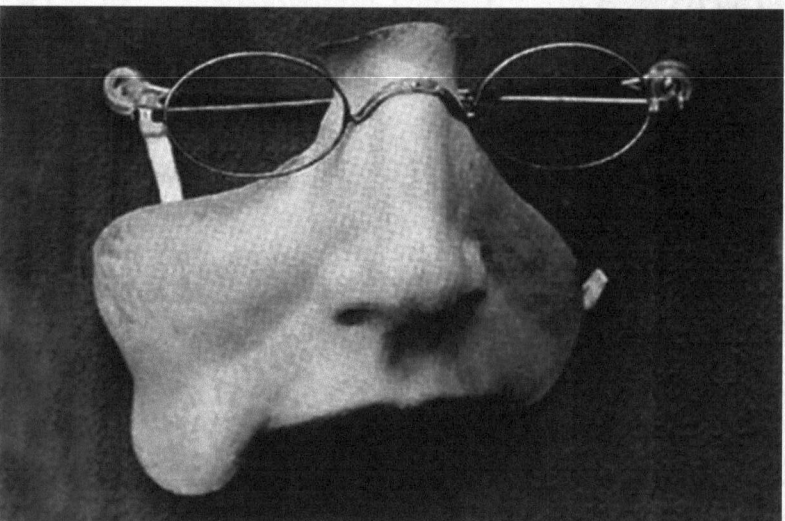

Sport was seen as a way of helping men recover. At Mayday Hospital in Surrey, for example, Colonel Deane set up a gymnastic exercise centre for disabled ex-servicemen. Many other hospitals had similar rehabilitation centres up and down the country. St Dunstan's Institute for the blind, now Blind Veterans UK, helped blind veterans to learn new skills such as typing, carpentry, basket making and shoe repairs to enable them to return to civilian life. Finding work was problematic for many disabled ex-servicemen, and some sheltered employment schemes were set up for their needs. Ex-servicemen trained as limb fitters at Roehampton Hospital, for example, and The Poppy Factory was opened providing employment for disabled veterans in the manufacture of, the now ubiquitous, artificial poppies. The *King's National Roll*, was a scheme set up in 1919, intended to encourage businesses to employ disabled ex-servicemen but, sadly, it had little success.

Top left, a German postcard publicising the Ludendorff Fund for disabled veterans, top right, a poster advertising for Polish land workers. Middle left, a disabled worker manufacturing artificial limbs, centre, a French labourer, middle left, two ex-servicemen. Bottom left, moulds used to make prosthetics for facial injuries, bottom right, a group of disabled ex-servicemen.

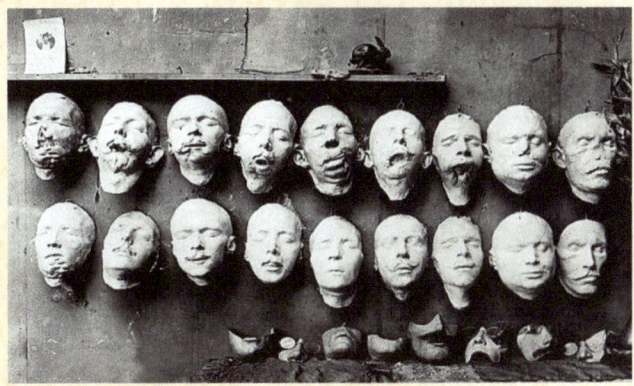

British war medals divide into two categories; campaign medals, awarded to all service personnel as well as to some civilians, for active wartime service and gallantry medals, awarded to individuals who distinguished themselves with notably courageous deeds. Over 300,000 such awards were bestowed on members of the British armed forces between 1914 and 1918.

The highest honour of all, the Victoria Cross, was awarded 628 times during the war. The youngest recipient was 16 year old, Jack Cornwell, who refused to leave his post despite suffering from fatal injuries during the Battle of Jutland. There have been only three men who have received the VC twice, two of whom earned a VC during The Great War.

Captain Noel Godfrey Chavasse VC & Bar, MC, a British medical doctor, was rescuing men in no man's land under constant sniper fire, in Guillemont in 1916, when he was hit by shell splinters. He gained a second VC rescuing men at Passchendaele. He was injured and died two days later of his wounds.

Surgeon-Captain Arthur Martin-Leake earned his first VC in 1902 during the Boer War. He was injured while treating wounded soldiers just yards from the enemy's line. He continued treating men until he collapsed from exhaustion, having first ordered that other wounded received water before he did. Martin-Leake's second VC was earned in 1914, near Zoonebeke in Belgium, rescuing men close to enemy lines, while under constant fire. Surgeon-Captain Arthur Martin-Leake died in 1953 aged 79.

During our research at the Imperial War Museum London, quite by chance, we met the grandson of Battery Sergeant Major George Dorrell, who was awarded the VC for his act of valour during an artillery action on 1st September 1914 at Nery, France. We found it a poignant experience to talk to him about his grandfather, and the action in which he won the award, whilst looking at his Victoria Cross.

The origins of the German Iron Cross, a black cross with a white or silver outline, dates back to 1219 when the Kingdom of Jerusalem granted the Teutonic Order the right to combine the Teutonic Black Cross placed above a silver Cross of Jerusalem.

The military decoration was first awarded in 1813 during the Napoleonic Wars. During The Great War, the Iron Cross 1st Class and the Iron Cross 2nd Class were awarded without regard to rank. Approximately 218,000 Iron Cross 1st Class, 5,196,000 Iron Cross 2nd Class and 13,000 non-combatant Iron Cross 2nd Class were awarded. Exact numbers of awards are not known, as the Prussian military archives were destroyed in World War II.

The Grand Cross was intended for senior generals of the Prussian, or later, German Army. An even higher decoration, the Star of the Grand Cross of the Iron Cross, was awarded only twice, to Generalfeldmarschall Gebhard Leberecht von Blücher in 1813 and to Generalfeldmarschall Paul von Hindenburg in 1918.

Iron Cross 2nd Class   Star of the Grand Cross Iron Cross

The war effectively came to an end when the armistice was signed between the Allied forces and Germany. This became known as the Armistice of Compiègne, named because of the location of the railway carriage where the documents were signed. The truce came into effect at 11 am European time on 11th November, 1918. Although not technically a surrender, the Germans were responding to the policies proposed by American president, Woodrow Wilson, in his *Fourteen Points* statement in January 1918.

Marshal of France, Ferdinand Foch, was the architect of the armistice. The terms included the cessation of hostilities, the withdrawal of German troops to behind their own borders, the preservation of infrastructure, the exchange of prisoners, the disposition of German warships and submarines, conditions for prolonging or terminating the armistice and a promise of reparations. It was the reparations that were to trigger another world event.

Although the armistice ended the actual fighting, it took six months of negotiations at the Paris Peace Conference to conclude the peace treaty; the Treaty of Versailles.

There was a post script to the armistice at Compiègne; a second armistice in the same railway carriage at the same location. Following the short yet decisive Battle of France in the spring of 1940, Adolf Hitler deliberately chose Compiègne Forest as the site where General Charles Huntziger was forced to sign the armistice on behalf of France. Hitler saw this symbolic action on the site of the 1918 Armistice as an act of revenge and humiliation.

Like a pebble thrown into a pool, the ripples of war continued, seeing dramatic political, cultural, and social change worldwide. The Austro-Hungarian, German, Ottoman and Russian empires collapsed due to the war and eight new countries were formed. Women gained the vote for the first time in history.

The seeds of the Second World War were sown at the end of the first. The Treaty of Versailles required Germany to pay billions of Deutschmarks in reparation for damage caused during the war. Hyperinflation began as presses worked overtime to print bank notes and by November, 1923 one US Dollar was worth 4,200,000,000,000 Deutschmarks. The German economy collapsed in 1931.

At the outbreak of war, Adolf Hitler volunteered to serve in the Bavarian Army. He was present at the First Battle of Ypres, the Battle of the Somme, the Battle of Arras, and the Battle of Passchendaele, and was wounded at the Somme. He was decorated for bravery, receiving the Iron Cross twice as well as the Black Wound Badge.

Hitler described the war as *the greatest of all experiences*. In 1925 he wrote *In these nights hatred grew in me, hatred for those responsible for the dead.* His wartime experience reinforced his patriotism and he was shocked by Germany's capitulation. His ideology began to take shape, he believed in the stab-in-the-back myth, which claimed that the German army, *undefeated in the field,* had been betrayed by civilian leaders and Marxists.

Whilst imprisoned at Landsberg for his political beliefs, Hitler wrote most of the first volume of *Mein Kampf.* The book laid out his plans for the transformation of German society based on race. Some passages implied genocide. Published in two volumes in 1925/6, it sold 228,000 copies between 1925 and 1932 and one million copies in 1933, his first year in power.

Sir Winston Churchill, KG, OM, CH, TD, DL, FRS, RA saw action as a young army officer in British India, the Sudan, and the Second Boer War. He gained fame as a war correspondent and wrote books about his campaigns.

In October 1911, Churchill was appointed First Lord of the Admiralty serving as both a politician and as an military officer until May 1915 when he rejoined the British Army, as a Major with the 2nd Battalion Grenadier Guards, then appointed Lieutenant-Colonel, commanding the 6th Battalion Royal Scots Fusiliers. As a commander he continued to exhibit the reckless daring which had been a hallmark of all his military actions, although he strongly disapproved of the mass slaughter involved in many Western Front actions.

In 1940, he became Prime Minister and remained so for the duration of the Second World War becoming highly regarded as one of the greatest wartime leaders of the 20th century. He was a well respected historian and writer, as well as an artist. He is the only British Prime Minister to have won the Nobel Prize for Literature and was the first person to be made an honorary citizen of the United States.

Joseph Stalin discovered the writings of Vladimir Lenin around 1899 and joined the Russian Social-Democratic Labour Party. Lenin formed the Bolsheviks and Stalin eagerly joined as an active member, distributing propaganda, provoking strikes, staging bank robberies, and ordering assassinations. Prior to the revolution of 1917, Stalin played an active role in fighting the Russian government. He took control of Pravda, a Russian political newspaper associated with the Communist Party. He then took a position in favour of supporting the provisional government. Stalin was appointed People's Commissar for Nationalities' Affairs, prompting a bitter civil war. In May 1918, Stalin started to impose his influence on the Soviet military. In 1919, in order to stem mass desertions on the Western Front, Stalin had deserters and renegades publicly executed as traitors.

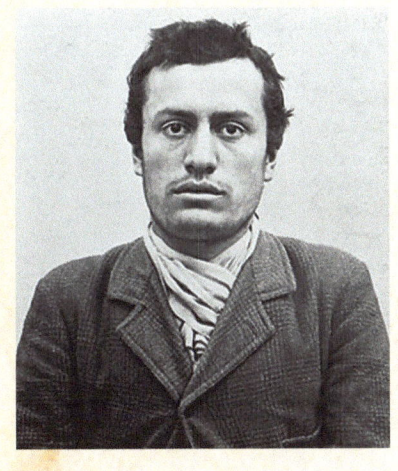
Benito Amilcare Andrea Mussolini, was expelled from the Italian Socialist Party for disagreeing with their war neutrality policy. In October 1914, he founded a newspaper, promoting Italy joining the war and formed *Fasci Rivoluzionari d'Azione Internazionalista*, which went on to be the fascist movement. Some of the finance for the fascists came from the French who were wanting him to join forces with them. He joined the Army, rising to the rank of corporal, and spent about nine months in the front line. In 1917, he was accidentally wounded by a mortar bomb explosion which finished his army career. On discharge from hospital, he resumed his editor-in-chief position at his newspaper. He was paid a weekly wage of £100, equivalent to £6000 today, from MI5, to publish pro-war propaganda. In October 1922, he became the youngest Prime Minister in Italian history and remained in that position until he was deposed in 1943.

At the age of sixteen, Hermann Wilhelm Göring, was sent to a military academy at Berlin Lichterfelde, from which he graduated with distinction. He joined the Prince Wilhelm Regiment in 1912. When war broke out he was stationed at Mulhouse, near the French border. A friend, Bruno Loerzer, convinced him to transfer to the air combat force of the German army. They flew reconnaissance and bombing missions, for which both received the Iron Cross, 1st class. On 7th July 1918, following the death of Wilhelm Reinhard, successor to Manfred von Richthofen, Göring was made commander of Jagdgeschwader 1, known more commonly as the *Flying Circus*. He had the reputation of being arrogant which made him unpopular with the men he served with. As a fighter pilot, he claimed 22 victories and received many medals including the coveted *Pour le Mérite*. Like many other German veterans, Göring believed that the German Army had not really lost the war, feeling betrayed by the civilian government, Marxists, Jews, and the Republicans, who had dismantled the German monarchy.

Blood Swept Lands and Seas of Red is an installation of 888,246 ceramic poppies at the Tower of London, created by ceramic artist Paul Cummins, with setting by stage designer, Tom Piper. Each poppy represents a British military fatality during the war. The poppies are being sold and the proceeds distributed between six service charities.

The Commonwealth War Graves Commission is responsible for 1.7 million people who died in the two world wars. They have 23,000 sites across 153 countries which are maintained

The brainchild of Sir Fabian Ware, the Commission was established, by Royal Charter, in 1917. Ware had been a commander of a British Red Cross mobile unit during the war and his unit started to record and look after graves that they came across. He was driven to ensure that the graves weren't lost in time and the men, and women, who died were always remembered.

Sir Herbert Baker, Sir Reginald Blomfield and Sir Edwin Lutyens, three of the most eminent architects at the time, were commissioned to design the cemeteries and memorials to the missing, and writer, Rudyard Kipling, was appointed as the literary advisor regarding the wording of the memorial inscriptions.

The Menin Gate Memorial, in Ypres, Belgium, is dedicated to the British and Commonwealth soldiers who were killed on the Ypres Salient and who have no known graves. The memorial is located at the starting point of one of the main roads out of the town that led Allied soldiers to the front line. Designed by Sir Reginald Blomfield, the Menin Gate Memorial was unveiled on 24th July 1927 when Field Marshal Lord Plumer said *He is not missing, he is here*. Since 2nd July 1928, apart from the duration of the Second World War, the Last Post has been played at the memorial every evening at 8pm.

The total number of military and civilian casualties in the war was over 37 million. There were over 16 million deaths and 20 million wounded. The total number of deaths includes about 10 million military personnel and about 7 million civilians. The Allies lost about 6 million military personnel while the Central Powers lost about 4 million. At least 2 million died from diseases and 6 million went missing, presumed dead.

War memorial to the men of Blaenporth and Aberporth, Ceredigion, Wales

The Grieving Parents, Käthe Kollwitz's memorial to her youngest son killed in 1914

MS Strange though it may sound to some, I have always found cemeteries captivating. I have many photographs of cemeteries, gravestones, war memorials and plaques from across the UK and abroad. I don't believe in the glorification of war but I strongly believe that we should always remember those who fought and died. My local town war memorial in March, Cambridgeshire, commemorates 228 men who died in World War One, as well as a further 103 who perished in World War Two. It is typical of a lot of urban war memorials across the country, a soldier in a mourning pose, sculpted in marble by Leominster based William G. Storr-Barber, with a granite obelisk mounted on a stepped plinth at a cost of £900.

War memorial in March, Cambridgeshire

French war memorial in Blagny, Ardennes

War memorial in Ingatestone, Essex

RS I think it important to remember that although the numbers of the injured and fallen in the Great War were colossal, the statistics reflect real individuals. Each person was loved for who they were, husband, wife, father, son, mother, daughter. Every community, large or small, made its own tribute to the fallen. In my home town of Chatteris, we have a memorial commemorating the 158 lives lost. Every community gave the lives of their young people in the hope of making a better world.

Chatteris War memorial

The conflict of the First World War has shaped the world we live in today. We owe a debt to all the people that sacrificed so much, we must remember the sacrifice they made and pass the stories down to the generations to come.

*Those who don't know history
are doomed to repeat it.*
Edmund Burke

No More Soldiering for Me

When this lousy war is over
No more soldiering for me
When I get my civvies clothes on
Oh, how happy I shall be
No more church parades on Sunday
No more asking for a pass
I shall tell the sergeant major
To stick his passes up his arse

When this lousy war is over
Oh how happy I shall be
When I get my civvie clothes on
And I return from Germany
I shall sound my own reveille
I shall make my own tattoo
No more N.C.O's to bollock me
No more rotten Army stew

N.C.O.'s will all be navvies
Privates ride in motor cars
Officers will smoke their Woodbines
Privates puff their big cigars
No more 'Stand-To' in the trenches
Never another church parade
No more shiv'ring on the fire step
No more Tickler's marmalade

No More Soldiering for Me, a parody on the hymn, *What a Friend We Have in Jesus,* was one of many songs which soldiers sung during the war. These bawdy and irreverent songs were often full of obscenities and anti-war sentiments. Many of the parodies were humorous at the expense of highly ranked officers. Rarely could these song lyrics be credited to any one person and there were many variations on the words. In such a punishing environment as the front line, these songs were morale boosting relief from everyday life in the trenches.

A Friendly Act by Richard Savage

Subject Index

Acoustic mirrors 37, 38,
Adolf Hitler 119
Aimee Byng Scott 25,
Amy Lowell 83
Animals 104 - 107
Archduke Ferdinand 1,
Armistice 118,
Aviation 62 – 68,
Baron von Richthofen 67,
Battle of the Somme 10,
Benito Mussolini 121
Bomb disposal 12,
Books 130
Bruce Bairnsfather 94
Captain Roy Brown 66,
Charlotte Mew 112,
Christmas 52, 56,
Christopher Nevinson 93,
Commonwealth War Graves Commission 123
Conscientious objectors 40,
Craiglockhart 86, 87, 88,
Edith Cavell 45
Environmental damage 15,
Ernest Hemingway 90,
Ernst Toller 6, 91,
Family 69, 70, 73,
Football 56, 58, 59
Gallipoli campaign 74, 75, 76
Gas 28, 30,
Gavrilo Princep 1
Georg Trakl 26, 27,
George Clare 72,
Harold Gillies 114,
Harry Betts 71,
Hermann Göring 121
Home front 78, 79, 84
Humour 47, 48, 50,
Imperial War Museum 116,
Iron Cross 117
Isaac Rosenberg 7, 22,
Ivor Gurney 9, 90,

Jane Bemrose 45
John McCrae 111,
John William Streets 74
Joseph Stalin 120
Kaiser Wilhelm 1,
Lawrence of Arabia 91,
Lice 22, 23, 24
Lochnagar Crater 11,
Lord Kitchener 2, 35,
Original artwork 1, 3, 7, 14, 15, 17, 20, 21, 23, 26, 29 - 31, 35, 43, 50, 57, 58, 62, 66, 67, 69, 75, 79, 82 - 84, 92, 97, 98, 100, 101, 109 - 111, 113, 127
Medical treatment 41, 42, 108, 114,
Nautical 60, 77, 96 – 99,
Nursing 44, 45, 77,
Otto Dix 93
Painters 93, 95,
Paul Nash 95,
Poetry 6, 7, 9, 18, 21, 22, 25, 27, 28, 74, 83, 89, 111, 112,
Poets 86 – 90,
Postal 54, 55,
Prisoners of War 102, 103
Rationing 84
Recruitment 2,
Resources 130
Rupert Brooke 89,
Shell shock 109, 110,
Siegfried Sassoon 86, 87, 88
Sniper trees 25,
Songs 65, 126
Suffrage 81,
Tanks 32, 33, 36,
Tower of London 122
Trench conditions 9, 17 - 19, 23, 24
USA 60, 61
Victoria Cross 40, 116,
War memorials 104, 123 - 125
Wilfred Owen 18, 21, 28, 87, 88,
Winston Churchill 120
Women 44, 45, 55, 77 - 81

Resources

BBC Archive
Blind Veterans UK
British Medical Journal
British Red Cross
Cambridgeshire Community Archive Network
Chatteris Museum
Commonwealth War Graves Commission
Gillies Archives
Imperial War Museum
IWM Duxford
IWM London
IWM War Memorials Archive
March Museum
Ministry of Defence
Tate Modern
The British Library
The British Postal Museum & Archive
The First World War Poetry Digital Archive
The Gallipoli Association
The Ministry of Defence Medal Office
The National Archives
The Royal British Legion
The Wellcome Collection
The Western Front Association
Victoria Cross Trust

A Selection of First World War Books

1914 Poetry Remembers edited by Carol Ann Duffy
A Farewell to Arms by Ernest Hemingway
A Stretcher Bearer's Diary by J. H. Newton
A War in Words by Svetlana Palmer & Sarah Wallis
All Quiet on the Western Front by Erich Maria Remarque
Animals in War by Jilly Cooper
Because You Died by Vera Brittain
Birdsong by Sebastian Faulks
Drawing Fire: The Diary of a Great War Soldier and Artist by Len Smith
Eleventh Month, Eleventh Day, Eleventh Hour: Armistice Day 1918
by Joseph E Persico
First World War Poems by Andrew Motion
First World War Posters by Rosalind Ormiston
Forgotten Lunatics of the Great War by Peter Barham
Forgotten Voices of the Great War by Max Arthur
Goodbye to All That by Robert Graves
Her Privates We by Frederic Manning
Life Class by Pat Barker
My Dear, I Wanted to Tell You by Louise Young
Parade's End by Ford Madox Ford
Private Peaceful by Michael Morpurgo
Regeneration trilogy (Regeneration, The Eye in the Door and The Ghost Road)
by Pat Barker
Scars Upon My Heart: Women's Poetry and Verse of the First World War by
Catherine Reilly
Shots from the Front: The British Soldier 1914 – 1918 by Richard Holmes
Silent Night: The Remarkable Christmas Truce of 1914 by Stanley Weintraub
Singled Out: How Two Million Women Survived Without Men After The First
World War by Virginia Nicholson
Somme by Lyn Macdonald
Stay Where You Are And Then Leave by John Boyne
Strange Meeting by Susan Hill
Stretcher Bearer: Fighting for Life in the Trenches by Charles H. Horton
Testament of Youth by Vera Brittain

The Collected Poems of Wilfred Owen by Wilfred Owen
The First Casualty by Ben Elton
The First Day on the Somme by Martin Middlebrook
The Flowers of the Field by Sarah Harrison
The Frightful First World War by Terry Deary
The Great War: A Photographic Narrative by The Imperial War Museum
The Guns of August by Barbara W Tuchman
The Missing of the Somme by Geoff Dyer
The Night Before Christmas 1914 by Richard Davis
The Road Back by Erich Maria Remarque
The Roses of No Man's Land by Lyn Macdonald
The Silver Donkey by Sonya Harknett
The War Poems by Siegfried Sassoon
The War Poems of Wilfred Owen by Wilfred Owen
The Wipers Times: The Complete Series of the Famous Wartime Trench Newspaper by Malcolm Brown
They Called It Passchendaele by Lyn MacDonald
To Hell and Back: The Banned Account of Gallipoli by Sydney Loch, includes a biography by Susanna & Jake de Vries
Toby's Room by Pat Barker
Tommy Rot: WW1 Poetry They Didn't Let You Read by John Sadler & Rosie Serdiville
Tommy: The British Soldier on the Western Front by Richard Holmes
Tommy's Ark: Soldiers and their Animals in the Great War by Richard van Emden
Trench Talk by Peter Doyle & Julian Walker
Up the Line to Death: War Poets 1914 – 1918 by Brian Gardner
VCs of the First World War The Air Vcs by Peter G. Cooksley & Peter F. Batchelor
Vimy by Pierre Berton
War Horse by Michael Morpurgo
Wilfred Owen: An Illustrated Life by Jane Potter & Jon Stallworthy
Woodbine Willie by Bob Holman
Wounded: From Battlefield to Blighty 1914 - 1918 by Emily Mayhew

They shall grow not old, as we that are left grow old:
Age shall not weary them, nor the years condemn.
At the going down of the sun and in the morning,
We will remember them.

            Laurence Binyon